United States Environmental Protection Agency	Enforcement and Compliance Assurance (2201A)	EPA/300-R-00-004 July 20, 2000 www.epa.gov/oeca/oej

Office of Environmental Justice

Environmental Justice in The Permitting Process:

A Report from the Public Meeting on Environmental Permitting Convened by the National Environmental Justice Advisory Council, Arlington, Virginia – November 30-December 2, 1999

National Environmental Justice Advisory Council

A Federal Advisory Committee to the U.S. Environmental Protection Agency

 **EPA**

NATIONAL
ENVIRONMENTAL JUSTICE
ADVISORY COUNCIL

August 3, 2000

Administrator Carol M. Browner
U. S. Environmental Protection Agency
1200 Pennsylvania Avenue, NW
Washington, DC 20460

Dear Administrator Browner:

Please find attached a copy of the report entitled "*Environmental Justice in the Permitting Process: A Report on the Public Meeting Convened by the National Environmental Justice Advisory Council, November 30-December 2, 1999.*"

The U.S. Environmental Protection Agency (EPA), through its Office of Environmental Justice, asked the National Environmental Justice Advisory Council (NEJAC) to provide advice and recommendations on the following question:

"In order to secure protection from environmental degradation for all citizens, what factors should be considered by a federal permitting authority, as well as state or local agencies with delegated permitting responsibilities, in the decision-making process prior to allowing a new pollution-generating facility to operate in a minority and/or low income community that may already have a number of such facilities?"

Clearly, this is a question that the Agency has wrestled with for some time. To address this question, NEJAC scheduled a three day public meeting of industry, government (federal, tribal, state, and local), academic, and community stakeholders to explore whether and how the issue of environmental justice could be integrated into the permitting process.

This report sets forth approximately eighty (80) policy proposals that were presented by representatives from various stakeholder groups. The breath of the discussions were exemplified by individuals and/or organizations that either provided comments, suggestions or recommendations on what EPA could and/or should consider in the permit review application process. The NEJAC has considered these policy proposals and has formulated the following recommendations. Consequently, NEJAC recommends that the Administrator undertake the following actions:

- Request the Office of General Counsel to clarify legal authority and provide guidance on, the extent to which, permit writers (including delegated state, tribal, and local governments) have a mandatory and/or discretionary authority to deny an environmental permit, condition a permit, or require additional permit procedures on environmental justice grounds.

- As delineated in EPA's 1997 Strategic Plan to ensure that all people, regardless of race, income or national origin, "are protected from significant risk to human health and the environment where they live, learn, and work," the NEJAC urges the Administrator to assert leadership in the quest to better understand the following: (1) cumulative impacts; (2) degree of risk; (3) community demographics; and (4) disproportionality of risk, and how these can be integrated into the permit review process, as appropriate.

- Strengthen and highlight public participation requirements which ensure that permit writers consult with affected communities on an ongoing and continuing basis (i.e., prior to the consideration or issuance of a permit) in the decision-making process.

- Ensure that federal environmental laws, policies, and guidance are fairly and equitably enforced among all communities so that environmental justice concerns can be fully integrated in federally adopted, approved, implemented or required environmental programs.

- Assert leadership by providing guidance for state, regional, local, and tribal governments on the environmental justice implications of permitting and siting decisions, and on the impact of local zoning ordinances on those decisions.

During the meeting, community stakeholders identified additional issues that they believed deserved consideration as factors in the permitting process. It should also be noted that industry stakeholders shared with other stakeholders a willingness to explore a variety of approaches to environmental justice in permitting. The NEJAC believes that the Agency should explore the multitude of thoughtful suggestions and recommendations outlined throughout the entire report.

The process for developing this report included the formation of a multi-stakeholder Working Group to assist Professor Fran Dubrowski, the principal author of this report, in her efforts to capture, compile, and edit the presentations and discussions that occurred during the NEJAC meeting. Also attached is a list of the names and affiliations of all those who served on this Working Group. We are pleased to present this report to you for your review, consideration, response and action.

Sincerely,

/signed/
Haywood Turrentine

/signed/
Vernice Miller-Travis

Haywood Turrentine
Chair, NEJAC

Vernice Miller-Travis
Chair, NEJAC Working Group

Attachments

NEJAC PERMITTING RECOMMENDATIONS WORKGROUP

Vernice Miller-Travis - Chair
Ford Foundation
New York, NY

Sue Briggum
WMX Technolgies
Washington, DC

Eileen Gauna
Southwestern University Law
School
Los Angeles, CA

Eugene Smary
Warner Norcross & Judd
Grand Rapids, MI

Samara Swanston
The Watchperson Project
Brooklyn, NY

Bill Swaney
Confederated Salish and
Kootenai Tribes
Pablo, MT

Dean B. Suagee
Vermont Law School
South Royalton, VT

Nathalie Walker

Earthjustice Legal Defense
Fund
New Orleans, LA

TIPS FOR THE READER

The references referred to in this report are coded as follows:

TR   Refers to the transcript page of the NEJAC plenary sessions conducted on November 30 and December 2, 1999, which are attached with this report. Each report page contains 4 transcript pages; e.g. I-5 appears on the 2nd page of the attachment.

R   Refers to the page number in the Pre-Meeting Report which is available as Appendix A on the EPA Web Site.

Appendices referenced in this report are not included as part of the printed copy but are available from EPA's website:
http://www.epa.gov/oeca/main/ej/nejacpub.html

Appendix A - Pre-Meeting Report (includes Stakeholder Interviews)
Appendix B - December 1999 NEJAC Executive Meeting Summary
Appendix C - NEJAC Air & Water Subcommittee Comments on the
                Draft Urban Air Toxics Strategy April 6, 1999
Appendix D – Transcripts from NEJAC Meeting
        I – November 30 Plenary Session is Attached
        II – December 1 Public Comment Session on EPA Web Site
        III – December 2 Plenary Session is Attached

TABLE OF CONTENTS

I.   BACKGROUND

EPA, through its Office of Environmental Justice, asked the National Environmental Justice Advisory Council (NEJAC) to provide advice and recommendations on the following question:

> In order to secure protection from environmental degradation for all citizens, what factors should be considered by a federal permitting authority, as well as state or local agencies with delegated permitting responsibilities, in the decision-making process prior to allowing a new pollution-generating facility to operate in a minority and/or low-income community that may already have a number of such facilities?

To address this question, NEJAC scheduled a three (3) day public meeting of industry, government (federal, tribal, state, and local), academic, and community stakeholders to explore whether and how the issue of environmental justice could be integrated into the permitting process. This gathering represented NEJAC's first public meeting to focus entirely on a single issue.

As a prelude to the meeting, the Office of Environmental Justice commissioned a report summarizing interviews with a representative sampling of stakeholders scheduled to participate in the public meeting. Twenty (20) stakeholders were interviewed: eight (8) representing EPA programs, three (3) representing industrial interests, three (3) representing academia, three (3) representing state or local governments, two (2) representing community organizations, and one (1) representing a Native American tribe. The pre-meeting report presented the responses of those stakeholders to a series of questions developed by the Office of Environmental Justice, identifying both potential areas of agreement as well as fundamental differences in perspective. (The Pre-Meeting Report, including a list of interviewed stakeholders and their organizational affiliations, can be found on the EPA Web Site as Appendix A.)

In general, stakeholders agreed on the need: (1) to address the issue of incorporating environmental justice concerns in permitting, (2) to define more clearly what the permit writer should do when confronted with disparate treatment, (3) to address cumulative impacts in some fashion (whether through permitting, regulation, or cooperation with land use agencies), and (4) to involve the community in permitting decisions. Stakeholders differed in their view: (1) of the appropriate overall Agency goal in permitting, and (2) of what now transpires in the permit process. R. 6-8, 10-16, 19-21.

For example, when asked whether the permit agency should address pre-existing conditions with potential health or environmental impacts in permitting, community stakeholders reply simply and emphatically *"Yes!"* They cited communities where *"shelter in place"* alarms are a regular feature of community life. *("Shelter in place"* refers to governmental strategies which seek to minimize human exposure to high air pollutant episodes by recommending residents go inside whenever an alarm whistle is sounded.) To community stakeholders, this signified that *"the system is broken.... There is no study which proves that "shelter in place" works, that [ordinary residential] structures adequately protect people...."* They stressed the need for meaningful planning and siting so that the number of people adversely affected in a worst-case pollution scenario is minimized or eliminated. R. 10.

State, local government, tribal, and academic stakeholders agreed that permit agencies should address pre-existing conditions. One emphasized these factors *"may be more important than sporadic permit issues."* Another added that such considerations *"should not be an afterthought, but should be raised early in the process and used as a guideline for determining whether any [siting] action should be taken at all."* A third concluded, *"A responsible agency looking out for the community's interests should relatively level the playing field."* R. 10.

Industry stakeholders approached this environmental justice goal more cautiously. They acknowledged *"agencies have to deal with cumulative risk in some fashion,"* but stressed the need for *"legal authority," "clear criteria for injustice," "enough information on emissions and health effects to make clear calls," "[and avoiding having] the system bog down."* They questioned whether *"agencies have the resources to have permit writers become fully conversant with these issues"* and emphasized that different perceptions on the issues may exist even within the local community, further complicating review. R. 11.

Nonetheless, industrial stakeholders shared with other stakeholders a willingness to explore approaches to environmental justice in permitting. While not endorsing any particular solution, industry stakeholders raised the following possibilities:

(1) Permit agencies can examine, document, and help raise awareness of pre-existing conditions.

(2) There could be further public scrutiny of zoning and land use planning for environmental justice impacts.

(3) Agencies could publicize more information on what factors contribute to successful brownfields projects.

(4) Rather than subject all permits -- even minor permits -- to full- blown cumulative impact analysis, agencies could screen permits to determine which merit fuller scrutiny because of the size of the source, toxicity of the emissions, or degree of public interest in the outcome.

(5) Corporate policies on siting and acquisition could be changed so that environmental personnel are integrated into decision-making earlier in the process, before companies are so heavily invested in a particular site. (Under current practice, siting is primarily market-driven. Only after a lengthy analysis of non-environmental factors, such as access to supplies and transportation corridors, growth potential, etc., does a company look at the community, its environment and quality of life.)

(6) Where high risks exist due to prior land use planning errors, successful relocation efforts and voluntary buy-outs could be examined. In the Netherlands, for example, when cumulative risk analysis indicated that community exposure crossed a specified threshold, the government devised a 5-10 year community relocation plan. Voluntary buy-outs to expand buffer zones around industrial facilities have also occurred in the United States. R. 11-12.

In general, EPA stakeholders agreed with the goal of addressing cumulative environmental impacts in permitting (assuming legal authority to do so). Some, however, expressed interest in limiting such analysis to major permits, "cancer alleys," or "hot spots," while others appeared to embrace it for a broader universe of permits. Several recommended greater attention to the environmental impacts of zoning and planning decisions, and other stakeholders concurred. R. 12.

Stakeholders also shared differing views as to what now transpires in the permit process. Industry stakeholders saw the current process as largely centered on technical issues of compliance with federal and state discharge regulations. Government stakeholders saw themselves addressing a somewhat broader set of issues -- still largely centered on compliance with technology requirements, but also encompassing public participation, protection of health and the environment, interagency coordination, enforcement, and state oversight. In marked contrast, tribal and community stakeholders saw the process as exceedingly narrow, ignoring treaty rights and community views -- indeed, driven toward a distinctly (from their view) biased result. One cited situations where facility construction is underway while the permit application is purportedly still being considered: *"Companies wouldn't invest this money if they didn't feel they could get their permit."* Another put it: *"The process proceeds with an eye toward nothing but technical compliance with numbers and, if there is not compliance, then how can we help the facility get its permit?"* At least one EPA stakeholder appeared to agree: *"If the objective [of the community] is to stop the permit altogether, ... it is hard for EPA to share that goal. Our goal is to make sure these sources have permits, unless they don't comply [with applicable regulations]."* R. 13.

All stakeholders, however, agreed that, absent a stronger or more comprehensive state statute, the current permit process does not address the type of environmental justice concerns being raised by tribal and community organizations. R. 13.

With respect to potential changes in the current permit process, accord among stakeholders was greatest on issues related to better public outreach, expanded community participation in decision-making, greater assurances of industry compliance, and greater attention to cumulative risks. Stakeholders differed more sharply over a community's right to prevent siting of a facility which otherwise complies with applicable regulatory standards. However, stakeholders acknowledged that these situations represent a small percentage of permit applications and can frequently be avoided by changed industry and government behavior (such as early involvement of environmental personnel in internal corporate decision-making and community representatives in government decision-making.) In short, stakeholders were optimistic about the possibility of identifying opportunities for mutual stakeholder gain. R. 10-16, 19-24.

At the meeting itself, the Office of Environmental Justice asked NEJAC to engage in a "robust policy dialogue" aimed at identifying both deficiencies in the current permit process and remedies or alternative approaches to permitting. Tr. I-40. Participants responded by identifying eighty (80) policy recommendations for implementation by EPA, other federal agencies, states, tribes, community organizations, and permit applicants. (A complete list of policy recommendations is outlined below in Section III of this report.)

These recommendations received varying degrees of consideration by NEJAC. Some reflected extensive deliberation by NEJAC subcommittees. The recommendations for siting and operating waste transfer stations, for example, were the product of a two (2) year review by NEJAC's Waste and Facility Siting Subcommittee. The Subcommittee toured waste transfer stations in two (2) cities (New York and Washington, D.C.) and gathered public testimony from numerous stakeholders, including private sector witnesses, community groups, and federal, state, and local officials. Their review culminated in a nearly fifty (50) page technical report accompanying their policy recommendation. Tr. III-143-146. The urban air toxic strategy recommendations likewise had been amply debated. NEJAC's Air and Water Subcommittee had culled over 200 recommendations to EPA during the rulemaking process; many of the Subcommittee's final recommendations have yet to be addressed and remain relevant during the implementation stage of the strategy. Tr. III-116-118. The NEJAC public meeting offered the various subcommittees a forum to present such findings and recommendations to a larger audience.

Other recommendations illustrated substantial academic research. Professor Yale Rabin from the Massachusetts Institute of Technology reported observations gleaned from thirty-five (35) years of scrutinizing disparities in delivery of municipal services to low-income and minority communities in at least sixty (60) locations throughout the United States. Tr. I-165-169. Professor Richard Lazarus from Georgetown University Law Center appended a draft law review article to his recommendations on legal factors in permitting. Tr. I-42-59. Again, the meeting presented an opportunity to highlight the product of such scholarly investigation.

Still other recommendations emerged from Agency representatives or from other stakeholders addressing NEJAC with their ideas -- sometimes for the first time -- at this public policy meeting.

Participants had an opportunity to outline the contours of a debate on the merits of at least some of these additional recommendations;[1] others were merely noted for future reference.

The primary purpose of *this* public meeting was a creative, wide-ranging identification of policy options rather than a resolution of the relative merits and disadvantages of each proposal. The Office of Environmental Justice promised participants a follow-up report which would serve as an interim step in the formation of NEJAC's strategic policy advice to the Agency. Tr. III-8-16. This report, therefore, aims to cull the recommendations, identify the specific actions requested or implied of EPA or other stakeholders, and present a decision document for NEJAC's review and action.

To facilitate further review by both NEJAC and EPA, this report groups the eighty (80) policy recommendations by key themes. Five (5) key themes emerged continually in stakeholders' discussions. These themes, and the recommendations related to them, affect *all* federal permit programs, regardless of media, location, or implementing agency. Since these themes form the premise of many of the more media-specific, geographically-based, or Agency-directed policy recommendations, these proposals are presented in detail, along with background information, in Section II below.

At the public meeting, NEJAC approved several of the policy recommendations contained in this report; any such approval has been noted alongside the recommendation and a copy of the relevant NEJAC resolution can be found in the December 1999 NEJAC Executive Summary on the EPA Web Page as Appendix B. The bulk of the recommendations, however, have yet to be debated fully by NEJAC. **It is important to stress, therefore, that the policy recommendations identified in this report do not represent the views of the Office of Environmental Justice, the author, or NEJAC itself. They are merely interim (albeit often extensively researched) suggestions for NEJAC's review and approval.** Indeed, a few (primarily those pertaining to streamlined, expedited permitting and emissions trading) could, without further clarification, be interpreted as mutually exclusive.

Several recommendations pertained to a single site. For example, NEJAC heard pleas to clean up Metales y Derivados, an abandoned site in Tijuana, and Condado Prestos in Ciudad Juarez, Tr. III-89, and to conduct a site assessment of the El Gato Negro site in Matamoros Tamaulipas, bordering Brownsville, Texas. Tr. III-90. Recommendations pertaining to single sites have not been included here, although NEJAC subcommittees will address these issues separately.

Finally, for a full understanding of the policy recommendations outlined below, this report should be read in conjunction with the Pre-Meeting Report and the December 1999 Executive Meeting Summary, which are located on the EPA Web Site as Appendix A and B. The pre-meeting report outlines how important the issue of environmental justice in permitting is, defines key stakeholder goals, and critiques the current permit process. In short, it explains *why* stakeholders desire policy reforms and *what* the general nature of those reforms should be. With that backdrop, this report begins to tackle the thorny question of *how* to achieve stakeholders' shared permit goals, whatever they may be.

Several of these policy recommendations come directly from stakeholder presentations; that is, stakeholders identified problems, formulated solutions to those problems, and articulated a clear methodology for accomplishing those solutions. Others emerged in a less direct fashion; stakeholders, acting as the story-tellers for communities with little political clout, voiced their frustrations, leaving it to policy analysts to shape their experiences into recommendations for Agency action. Wherever possible, these experiences, too, have been outlined in the form of implied remedies, so that the recommendations before the Agency reflect the full range of stakeholder insights presented at the meeting.

---

[1] See, for example, the EPA Air Program's proposal for permit flexibility in communities with proactive emission reduction programs and some stakeholders' reservations. Cf. Tr. I-140-148, III-25, 29-46 with Tr. I-145-148, 227-228, 271-272, 318, 327-332, III-41-45, 59, 62-64, 113-114, 163, 167-178.

II.   KEY POLICY RECOMMENDATIONS.

Five (5) key themes surfaced repeatedly in both stakeholder interviews and public testimony. These concerned: (1) the need to clarify what legal authority the permit writer has to address environmental justice issues in permitting; (2) substantive permit criteria (including cumulative impacts, degree of risk, community demographics, and disproportionality of risk); (3) community involvement in the decision-making process; (4) enforcement; and (5) the relationship between land use/zoning and environmental decisions. This section of this report discusses each in turn.

A. Legal Authority to Address Environmental Justice Issues in Permitting.

Background:

Because permit writers implement statutes and regulations, the need to clarify the permit writer's legal authority to address environmental justice issues in permitting emerged as a primary stakeholder concern in both pre-meeting interviews and in testimony at the public meeting. See R. 20-21 and Tr. I-234-240, 247-249, 264.

In pre-meeting interviews, government stakeholders frequently cited their lack of authority to reject projects on environmental justice grounds. R. 20. At the public meeting, too, NEJAC heard repeated testimony that many permit writers believe they lack any legal authority to address environmental justice concerns in permitting decisions. Tr. I-46-47. Others believe that environmental justice concerns may form a basis for more exacting technical scrutiny of a permit, but are insufficient to deny an application which otherwise complies with media-specific technical criteria. Tr.I-205-208.

Confusion at the federal level is compounded in state and local permit agencies. When federal agencies fail to address environmental justice concerns, essential environmental decisions are left to states and local governments, which, in turn, fear tackling them because of potential "takings" lawsuits pursuant to the "just compensation" clause of the Fifth Amendment to the U.S. Constitution. Tr. I-182-183, 251-253. In addition, existing federal and/or state laws may preempt local authority to regulate. Tr. I-184. (Many states have laws prohibiting state agencies from issuing requirements more stringent than federal requirements.) Then too, in the absence of clear federal rules or guidelines, states fear being overturned in court for being "arbitrary and capricious" if they deny a permit on environmental justice grounds. Tr. I-204-208. As one state official explained: *"We are looking to EPA for the tools on how to do this."* Tr. I-262-264, R. 8.

Industry stakeholders, too, are uncertain of their obligations (beyond the need to avoid intentional discrimination). An industry stakeholder summarized, *"On the substance, there is real intellectual bankruptcy. What are the rules of the road? What does the Executive Order forbid? What is the basis of a Title VI complaint? What is the right thing to do? Companies fear that projects will be abandoned or delayed without reason and that others will go forward where they shouldn't.... There is no coherent understanding of what we're trying to do."* R. 20-21. In short, stakeholders from government, the private sector, academia, and community groups agree that legal clarification is a high priority.

The issue is becoming ever more prominent as permitting provisions of federal environmental laws increase in practical significance; whereas once only the Clean Water Act depended primarily on individual facility permits for implementation, now the Clean Air Act, the Resource Conservation Recovery Act, and the Safe Drinking Water Act have matured into permitting statutes. Tr. I-47.

In 1996, EPA's Office of General Counsel prepared a document identifying nine (9) federal statutes, including the Clean Air Act, Clean Water Act, Superfund, and RCRA, as providing opportunities

9

to incorporate environmental justice issues into permit decisions. Tr. I-48-51, 237-240 and 247-248. NEJAC responded by adopting a resolution calling upon EPA to utilize more systematically existing statutory authority to address environmental justice through permitting decisions. Tr. I-48-49. In response, EPA regional offices made sporadic efforts to reform permitting practices, but stakeholders saw little systematic effort by EPA Headquarters to develop a coherent set of guidelines promoting environmental justice permitting practices. Tr. I-49. Hence, three (3) years later, the status of the Office of General Counsel memorandum and the extent to which permit writers may honor its suggestions appears uncertain. Tr. I-247-249, 264.

Thus, permit writers face two (2) separate, seemingly unresolved questions: 1) under what circumstances, if any, does a permitting agency have a duty to deny or condition a permit on environmental justice grounds; and 2) if there is no mandatory duty, when, if ever, does an agency have discretion to act? On the latter point, several legal commentators noted that important Agency initiatives have often occurred in the statutory interstices, where EPA has discretion but no binding mandate. So not only is there precedent for such an approach, but, indeed, this is where EPA historically exerts its leadership in crafting an environmental agenda. Tr. I-50-55, 223-224, 249. Certainly, as Professor Lazarus noted, recent decisions of the EPA Environmental Appeals Board suggest there may be circumstances where EPA is called upon to exert similar leadership with respect to environmental justice concerns. Tr. I-55.

Community stakeholders criticized the Agency for not using existing statutory authority creatively. R. 20. Some also argued that the wording of EPA's question to NEJAC (i.e., "what factors should be considered ... prior to allowing a new pollution-generating facility to operate") *"presumes the permitting agency will allow a new pollution-generating facility in an already burdened community."* Tr. I-234-235, 251-253. These advocates warned against recommendations limited solely to process (i.e., to the inclusion of community comment and consultation) rather than to substantive environmental remedies and argued that EPA's inquiry should be open to the possibility that environmental justice concerns constitute valid bases for *denying* a permit altogether. Indeed, one community representative pointed out that EPA, unlike the Nuclear Regulatory Commission, had never denied a permit on environmental justice grounds. Tr. I-235-236. The Nuclear Regulatory Commission, by contrast, found racial bias in the site selection process and reversed a staff licensing decision on that basis in the case of *In re* Louisiana Energy Services, L.P., 24 N.R.C. 77 (1998). Tr. I-256.

Industry stakeholders found this comparison imprecise, noting that EPA and States may advise an applicant not to apply for a permit or to stop an application mid-process, thereby avoiding the need for permit denial. Tr. I-254-256. Thus, the number of permit denials, by itself, may not reflect the true impact of environmental justice concerns in permitting.

Where the applicant still wants to proceed, however, the question is a key one because it goes to the weight to be given environmental justice concerns. Are environmental justice-related factors, on the one hand, merely factors to be studied, there to contribute to the quality of decision-making and, in appropriate circumstances, to dissuade a reasoned agency or permittee from proceeding? Or do environmental justice-related factors hold somewhat greater weight, increasing the scope of required mitigation but, again, lacking sufficient weight to delay or forestall a project? Or -- and this is the ultimate test of their import -- do environmental justice-related factors have the ability to stop a project altogether? In other words, can a project which otherwise complies with all applicable environmental criteria be denied a permit solely because the project would put undue strain on an already overburdened community? At the public meeting or in pre-meeting interviews, stakeholders from virtually every interest group recommended that EPA squarely address these questions, which are subsumed within the overarching question posed by EPA's Office of Environmental Justice.

The EPA Administrator should request the Office of General Counsel to provide legal guidance to federal, as well as delegated state, tribal, and local government permit writers on whether they have either a mandatory duty or discretionary authority to deny a permit, condition a permit, or require additional permit procedures on environmental justice grounds. Specifically, the Office of General Counsel should address the following questions posed, either in remarks or in prepared material, to NEJAC at the public meeting by academicians and lawyers representing community groups:

1. Does the Rio Declaration on the Environment and Development, which the United States adopted in 1992, impose a mandatory duty on EPA, or provide discretionary authority, to address the potential effects of long-term exposure to multiple low-level toxins in permitting facilities in close proximity to environmental justice communities?

    Principle 15 of the Rio Declaration commits signatory governments to adopt a precautionary approach toward environmental hazards:

    "In order to protect the environment, the precautionary approach shall be widely applied by States according to their capabilities. Where there are threats of serious or irreversible damage, lack of full scientific certainty shall not be used as a reason for postponing cost-effective measures to prevent environmental degradation." Tr. I-239-240 and attachments.

2. Does the International Convention on the Elimination of All Forms of Racial Discrimination, ratified by the United States in 1994 and made applicable to executive agencies, including EPA, by Executive Order 13107 in 1998, impose a mandatory duty on EPA, or provide discretionary authority, to address environmental justice concerns in permitting?

    The International Convention requires signatory governments to:

    "take effective measures to review governmental, national, and local policies, and to amend, rescind, or nullify any laws and regulations which have the effect of creating or perpetuating racial discrimination wherever it exists."

    Executive Order 13107 directs *"all executive departments and agencies [such as EPA] ...shall maintain a current awareness of United States international human rights obligations that are relevant to their functions and shall perform such functions as to respect and implement those obligations fully."*
    Tr. I-239-240 and attachments.

3. Does the National Environmental Policy Act (NEPA) require or authorize EPA to undertake a comprehensive environmental impact review of permits in environmental justice communities? Tr. I-170-171.

    NEPA and its implementing regulations require federal agencies to explain the need for any proposed project which significantly affects the quality of the human environment, analyze all reasonable alternatives to the proposal, evaluate the "no action" alternative, and assess all impacts, including cumulative, indirect, and socioeconomic impacts. Ordinarily, federal permitting must comply with NEPA, but courts have exempted most EPA permits by the "functional equivalent doctrine" (i.e., the notion that, since EPA is primarily an environmental agency, EPA accomplishes the same analysis as NEPA-type environmental impact assessments).

The distinction is significant. The Nuclear Regulatory Commission remanded a nuclear material license where it found inadequate consideration of environmental justice concerns. In re Louisiana Energy Services, L.P., 47 N.R.C. 77 (1998) Tr. I-256. Some states, such as California, require similar NEPA-type analysis of major permit applications and these analyses can elicit information about significant health and environmental issues. Tr. I-195.

4. Does the Clean Air Act authorize or require EPA (and states administering EPA-delegated programs) to take environmental justice concerns into consideration in the permitting process? Relevant provisions cited in a law review article presented to NEJAC include:

- National ambient air quality standards (and revisions to the standards) must protect the public health of *especially sensitive subpopulations. See, e.g.*, American Lung Assn. v. EPA, 134 F.3d 388, 389 (D.C. Cir. 1998). (Environmental justice communities frequently include many individuals with heightened sensitivity to pollutants due to pre-existing physical conditions or environmental stresses from multiple sources.)

- State implementation plans to attain and maintain national ambient air quality standards must not conflict with any provision of federal law, including, presumably, *Title VI* of the Civil Rights Act. *See* section 110(a)(2)(E), 42 U.S.C. 7410(a)(2)(E).

- Permits in attainment areas must follow "careful evaluation of *all* the consequences of such a decision." Section 160, 42 U.S.C. 7470(5) (emphasis added).

- Permits in attainment areas must follow "adequate procedural opportunities for informed public participation in the decision-making process," including a public hearing offering interested parties an opportunity to appear and comment on "*alternatives*" and "*other appropriate considerations*" in addition to air quality impacts and emission controls. Sections 160 and 165A2, 42 U.S.C. 7470 and 7475(emphasis added). Tr. I-237.

- Sanctions for failure to attain national air quality standards include "all measures that can be feasibly implemented in the area in light of technological achievability, costs, and any *nonair quality* and other air quality-related health and environmental impacts." Section 179(d)(2), 42 U.S.C. 7509(d)(2)(emphasis added).

- Permits for sources in nonattainment areas may only be issued if "an analysis of alternative sites, sizes production processes, and environmental control techniques for such proposed source demonstrates that benefits of the proposed source significantly outweigh the environmental *and social costs imposed as a result of its location*, construction, or modification." Section 173(a)(5), 42 U.S.C. 7503(a)(5)(emphasis added).

12

- Section 112(r)(7) also authorizes the EPA Administrator to consider *location and response capabilities* in establishing requirements to prevent accidental releases of hazardous air pollutants. 42 U.S.C. 7412(r)(7).

- Requirements for the siting of solid waste incinerators must "minimize, on a *site specific* basis, to the maximum extent practicable, *potential risks* to public health or the environment." Section 129(a)(3), 42 U.S.C. 7429(a)(3)(emphasis added).

- Penalties for noncompliance with applicable Clean Air Act provisions must reflect "such other factors as *justice* may require," including, presumably, the potentially *greater need for deterrence* in communities which have historically lacked the resources to oversee facility compliance. *See* section 113(e)(1), 42 U.S.C. 7413(e)(1)(emphasis added).

- EPA has broad discretion to impose whatever permit conditions "are necessary to assure compliance." Section 504, 42 U.S.C. 7661c. Conceivably, permit conditions could include provisions to enhance a community's ability to oversee facility compliance.

- Finally, state boards with responsibility for permitting and enforcement of the Act must have "at least a majority of members who represent the *public interest.*" Section 128, 42 U.S.C. 7428(emphasis added). The "public interest" standard may allow EPA to require that such boards include representatives of environmental justice communities.

5. Does section 112(k) of the Clean Air Act, 42 U.S.C. 7412(k), require or authorize EPA (and delegated permit authorities) to address environmental justice concerns about cumulative burdens and their associated health risks in urban areas?

Section 112(k) addresses hazardous air pollutants from "area sources" (i.e., stationary sources that are not major) that individually *or collectively* present significant risks to public health in urban areas. The section directs EPA to monitor for a broad range of hazardous air pollutants, analyze contributing sources, and assess the public health risks they pose. EPA also must develop a comprehensive national emission control strategy, encourage and support State and local emission control strategies, and report to Congress on specific metropolitan areas that continue to experience high risks to public health from area source emissions. *See also* section 112(c)(3), 42 U.S.C. 7412(c)(3) and Tr. I-294-295.

6. Does the Resource Conservation and Recovery Act ("RCRA") require or authorize EPA (and delegated permit authorities) to address such environmental justice concerns as cumulative risk, unique exposure pathways, and sensitive populations? Tr. I-238. Relevant provisions cited in a law review article presented to NEJAC include:

- Standards applicable to generators and transporters of hazardous waste as well as hazardous waste treatment, storage, and disposal facilities must incorporate such protective requirements "*as may be necessary to protect human health and the environment,*" language broad enough to encompass consideration of cumulative impacts. *See* sections 3002(a), 3003(a), and 3004(a), 42 U.S.C. 6922(a), 6923(a), and 6924(a)(emphasis added).

- Permits for hazardous waste treatment, storage, or disposal facilities "shall contain such terms and conditions as the Administrator (or the State) determines *necessary to protect human health and the environment.*" Section 3005(c)(3), 42 U.S.C. 6925(c)(3)(emphasis added). EPA's own Environmental Appeals Board has read this language to allow the Agency to "tak[e] a more refined look" at health and environmental impacts which disproportionately affect a low-income or minority population. *See In re* Chemical Waste Management, Inc., 1995 WL 395962 (E.P.A. June 29, 1995).

- Standards applicable to hazardous waste treatment, storage, and disposal facilities "shall specify criteria for the *acceptable location* of new and existing treatment, storage, and disposal facilities as necessary to protect human health and the environment." Section 3004(o)(7), 42 U.S.C. 6924(o)(7)(emphasis added). *See also* section 3004(a)(4), 42 U.S.C. 6924(a)(4). Defining an "acceptable location" from a human health perspective presumably permits the Agency to account for environmental justice concerns regarding risk aggregation.

- Enforcement penalties must take into account the *"seriousness* of the violation." Section 3008(a)(3), 42 U.S.C. 6928(a)(3)(emphasis added). Violations can be more serious when risks are aggregated, disproportionate, or inequitable, or when risks impact an especially sensitive community.

- Guidelines for state solid waste management plans must consider *"the political, economic, organizational, financial, and management problems* affecting comprehensive solid waste management." Section 4002 (c)(9), 42 U.S.C. 6942(c)(9) (emphasis added). These factors are sufficiently broad to encompass many environmental justice concerns.

7. Does the Clean Water Act authorize or require EPA (and delegated states) to assess cumulative risk? Relevant provisions cited in a law review article presented to NEJAC include:

- Water quality standards under the Act must protect both public health and the "designated use" of each individual waterbody. Sections 302, 303, and 304, 33 U.S.C. 1312, 1313, and 1314. "Designated uses" could include economic or cultural uses (such as subsistence fishing or uses reflecting tribal traditions).

- The statute requires watershed protection, which, in turn, requires gathering loading data and evaluating pre-existing environmental stressors. *See* section 303(d), 33 U.S.C. 1313(d), and Tr. I-237, 243-244.

- Until all implementing actions have been taken under the statute, the Act gives EPA broad authority to condition discharge permits on *"such conditions as the Administrator determines are necessary* to carry out the provisions of this chapter." *See* section 402(a), 33 U.S.C.

1342(a)(emphasis added). These permit conditions could include provisions promoting environmental justice.

- Finally, civil and administrative penalties for violations of the Act must be based on the seriousness of the violation and "such other matters as *justice* may require." Section 309(d) and (g), 33 U.S.C. 1319(d) and (g)(emphasis added).

8. Do the Safe Drinking Water Act, Toxic Substances Control Act, and Federal Insecticide, Fungicide, and Rodenticide Act require or authorize EPA to address environmental justice concerns in permitting? Relevant provisions cited in a law review article presented to NEJAC include:

- The Safe Drinking Water Act directs EPA to set national primary drinking water regulations after considering, among other things, "*other factors relevant* to protection of health." Section 300g-1(b)(7)(C)(1), 42 U.S.C. 1412 (b)(7)(C)(1)(emphasis added). Cumulative impacts in environmental justice communities would seem to be such a relevant factor.

- State variances from national primary drinking water regulations for public water systems "shall be conditioned on such *monitoring and other requirements* as the Administrator may prescribe," including, presumably, enhanced public participation opportunities and resource assistance where appropriate in environmental justice communities. *See* section 300g-4(a)(1)(B), 42 U.S.C. 1415(a)(1)(B)(emphasis added).

- Civil penalties for violations of the Safe Drinking Water Act shall consider "the seriousness of the violation" and "such other matters as *justice* may require." Section 300h-2(c)(4)(B), 42 U.S.C. 1423 (c)(4)(B)(emphasis added).

- The Toxic Substances Control Act directs EPA to consider "*cumulative or synergistic effects*" in setting testing requirements for chemical substances and mixtures -- precisely the effects environmental justice advocates contend have been too often overlooked in considering the risks posed by toxic substances in low-income and minority communities. *See* section 4(b)(2)(A), 15 U.S.C. 2603(b)(2)(A).

- The Toxic Substances Control Act further directs EPA to consider the "environmental, economic, and *social impact* of any action" taken under the Act. Section 2(c), 15 U.S.C. 2601(c)(emphasis added).

- Finally, the Toxic Substances Control Act targets "*low-income persons*" for technical and grant assistance in State radon programs. Sections 305(a)(6) and 306(i)(2), 15 U.S.C. 2665(a)(6) and 2666(i)(2).

- The Federal Insecticide, Fungicide, and Rodenticide Act gives EPA broad authority to prevent "unreasonable adverse effects" on the environment, including effects on farmworkers. *See* section 3(a), 7 U.S.C. 136a(a).

9.   Finally, to what extent must states, tribes, and local governments administering delegated programs adhere to the same restrictions and, to the extent that they must, should these requirements be embodied in rulemaking? This question of rulemaking is important, not only to bind states, tribes, and local governments, but also to protect them from suits alleging that they are "arbitrary and capricious" when they deny a permit on environmental justice grounds. Tr. I-204-208.

B. Substantive permit criteria.

Background:

EPA's 1997 Strategic Plan commits the Agency to ensure that "all Americans are protected from significant risk to human health and the environment where they live, learn, and work." The same Strategic Plan binds the Agency to enforce all federal laws protecting human health and the environment "fairly and effectively." Finally, the Plan guarantees that all segments of society have access to information sufficient to participate effectively in managing health and environmental risk." Tr. I-16-17.

Despite these assurances, NEJAC heard repeated and compelling testimony from a multiplicity of low-income and minority communities that
polluting sources are being located in sufficient proximity to residential areas and/or to each other to form cancer alleys, cancer hotspots, or other health risks. As Professor Lazarus explained, *"Risks that may seem acceptable in isolation may properly be seen as presenting unacceptably high risks when the broader social context, including associated health and environmental risks, is accounted for in total aggregation."* Tr. I-45.

Where such conditions exist, permit writers remain confused as to whether they can address such risks, how to address them (assuming they have legal authority to do so), and even which of many different types of aggregate risks to consider.

Recommendation:

The EPA Administrator should direct permit writers to issue only permits consistent with EPA's mission; namely, protecting the health of all citizens. Specifically, permit writers should ensure that any permit: a) complies with all applicable provisions of law, including state and local health, environmental, and zoning laws (where such laws are not preempted), and b) adequately protects health and the environment. Specific factors which academicians and community groups believe the Agency should consider in determining the bases for modifying or denying permits in low-income or minority communities include:

(1) negative health risks;
(2) racially disproportionate burdens;
(3) cumulative and synergistic adverse impacts on human health and the environment;
(4) high aggregation of risk from multiple sources;
(5) community vulnerability based on the number of children, elderly, or asthmatics;
(6) cultural practices, including Tribal and indigenous cultures and cultural reliance on land and water that may become pathways of toxic exposure;
(7) proximity to residential areas and adequacy of buffer zones;
(8) health and ecological risk assessment;
(9) the economic burden of medical costs and lost productivity;
(10) access to health care;
(11) psychological impacts;

(12) the risk of chemical accidents;

(13) emergency preparedness;

(14) community right-to-know in permitting;

(15) the impact on the quality of life in the surrounding community; and

(16) an applicant's compliance history. Tr. I-45-46, 195, 225-227, 234-237, 240-246, 250-251, 268, 271-272, 281-282, 293-296, 301, 318, III-20-23, 50-59, 77-85, R. 10-11, 13-14.

Business and state stakeholders emphasized that, if EPA decides to incorporate such factors in the permitting process, it must do so through rulemaking in order to ensure that the terms are clearly understood and uniformly employed. Tr. I-206-208, 218-219, R. 11, 18, and 20-21. Community groups and some academicians, by contrast, stress that EPA could use existing regulatory authority more creatively to accomplish this end. Tr. I-46-51, 169-173, 181, 187, 237, and 247-249. At least one business representative also suggested that, if EPA incorporates such factors in permitting, it screen permits to determine which merit fuller scrutiny because of the size of the source, toxicity of the emissions, or degree of public interest in the outcome. R. 12.

(Additional recommendations on appropriate substantive permit standards and siting criteria are contained in Section III below.)

C. Community involvement/public participation

Background:

Non-Agency stakeholders agree that one of the most serious -- and easily remedied flaws -- in current permitting is the way environmental agencies fail to engage the public in permit decision-making. Tr. III-13, 22, R. 14-16. The issue is a key one because inadequate public comment processes generate community mistrust, delay or disrupt industry plans, and impair agency decision-making. Indeed, EPA Administrator Carol M. Browner stressed to NEJAC that when permit agencies succeed in engaging a local community in a meaningful manner, the quality of the Agency's environmental decision-making is dramatically improved. Tr. I-106. Stakeholders generated a wealth of suggestions for improving the public participation process, most of which centered on the concept that consultation with potentially affected communities should occur "early and often."

Recommendation:

The EPA Administrator should adopt binding public participation requirements which ensure that permit writers will consult with affected communities "early and often." Tr. I-87-88, 91-99, 129-130, 198-199, R. 14-16, 19-20. Specifically, these requirements should direct permit agencies to:

a. Contact potentially affected communities as soon as an agency is aware that a permit application may be filed or that emissions from a facility may increase, but in no event later than immediately upon receipt of the permit application or notice that emissions could increase. Tr. I-91-92, 129-130, 132-133, 198-199, R. 19.

b. Hold an initial hearing or informal meeting with the potentially affected communities immediately after receipt of a permit application. This will afford an early opportunity to apprise the community of the pendency of the application, identify community concerns, avoid the mistrust created by prolonged agency and industry negotiations outside the public eye, and establish a basis for an ongoing, credible dialogue. R. 14-16, 19-22.

c. Identify community leaders accurately; do not rely on local government to represent environmental justice communities, because many low-income and/or minority communities do not have local visibility or political influence. Tr. I-129-130.

d. Develop a plan for community involvement in conjunction with the community. Tr. I-91-92.

e. Require a community outreach plan modelled on those used with success in the brownfields grants program; follow up to ensure that the plan is implemented. Tr. I-131-132, R. 12.

f. Use broadcast media and other effective forms of communication to advertise the public participation process. Tr. I-94-95, R. 19.

g. Require permit notices in newspapers to be printed in legible print and to be placed in spots likely to attract the attention of affected residents. Tr. I-82-83, 355. (Community stakeholders persistently criticized notices which are printed: solely in the Federal Register or state equivalent, in publications not read by the community, or in obscure legal notices and other fine print. R. 14.)

h. In public notices of proposed permits, describe what the discharge/emission means to the community in lay, rather than technical, terms. Otherwise, comment periods end before communities learn about potential impacts. Tr. I-87-88, 101-103, 132-133, III-20, R. 14.

i. Utilize local government resources as well by bringing local government into the process as early as possible. Tr. I-95-97, 187-189.

j. Make technical reports accessible to the community as soon as they are available, rather than holding them internally until commencement of a 30-day comment period. Community stakeholders criticized the 30-day comment period as an inadequate time in which to obtain independent technical advice on the complicated issues involved in permitting. (Presumably, this recommendation would require agencies to establish a publicly accessible permit docket.) Tr. I-132-133, R. 14.

k. Extend the 30-day public comment period for complicated permits. Tr. I-132-135.

(Additional recommendations on community involvement are outlined in Section III below.)

D. Enforcement.

Stakeholders recognized an integral relationship between permitting and enforcement. As several stakeholders repeatedly emphasized, permit writers need to think about how enforceable their permits will be, while enforcers need to rely on the permits to ground their prosecutions. Tr. I-359, III-25-26, 62-63.

The EPA Administrator should ensure that environmental justice guidance and requirements are effectively enforced in federally adopted, approved, or required environmental programs. Specifically, the Administrator should:

1. Ensure that EPA guidance on environmental justice reaches beyond the headquarters level to each of the regional offices and, in particular, regional permit writers. Tr. I-155-160, 277.

2. Ensure that EPA guidance on environmental justice reaches beyond to state personnel, especially permit writers, administering federally approved or required programs. Tr. I-160.

3. Assess all delegated state permit programs for compliance with federal legal requirements and withdraw federal program delegation in states which fail to implement the requirements. Tr. I-84, 102.

4. Address unpermitted or underpermitted activity, since this is a major problem. Tr. I-144, III-62-63.

5. Be more assertive in exercising regulatory authority to reopen permits for grandfathered facilities, many of which would not have been approved under modern standards. Tr. I-169-170.

6. Use enforcement programs to capture the economic benefits of permit violations so that corporations cannot profit from pollution. (See the NEJAC Enforcement Subcommittee's resolution and report on "Credible Deterrence," which can be found in Appendix B on the EPA Web Site) . Tr. III-164-165.

(Additional recommendations concerning enforcement are outlined in Section III of this report.)

E. Land use/zoning.

Background:

The relationship of land use and zoning to environmental justice was highlighted by the presentation of Professor Yale Rabin from the Massachusetts Institute of Technology. Professor Rabin reported observations gleaned from thirty-five (35) years of scrutinizing disparities in delivery of municipal services to low income and minority communities in at least sixty (60) locations throughout the United States. He noted that many pre-existing environmental injustices in minority and low-income communities can be traced to racially discriminatory local government actions -- actions taken in *compliance* with local zoning ordinances and compounded by other government policies.

For example, racially discriminatory real estate covenants were widely used before the adoption of comprehensive zoning. These covenants restricted minorities to certain geographic locations, which were then the host sites for polluted or undesirable land uses. The rigidly controlled boundaries of these neighborhoods caused severe overcrowding. Later, comprehensive zoning (mainly but not exclusively in the south) designated existing black residential areas as the site for further industrial or commercial growth. Because these residentially incompatible but permitted uses resulted in the frequent displacement of black residents, Dr. Rabin dubbed this phenomenon "expulsive zoning." In other words, comprehensive zoning had an *opposite* result in white and black neighborhoods. In white neighborhoods, zoning prevented intrusive traffic, noise, and pollution; in black neighborhoods, zoning induced such nuisances. These origins, though not widely understood, are important to note to the extent that current policy-makers are tempted to rely on local zoning to alleviate environmental injustice.

Compounding the zoning impact, municipalities frequently permitted substandard construction in minority neighborhoods -- in violation of town building code requirements governing adequate living space, lot size, ventilation, electricity, water supply, and sanitation. In addition, local governments, again especially in the south, often failed to provide municipal services such as paved streets, streetlights, storm and sanitary sewers, fire hydrants, and adequate water supply to black neighborhoods. Thus, although the racially discriminatory local government actions that generated these conditions have long since been mainly discontinued, the consequences remain in probably thousands of black neighborhoods. Tr. I-165-169, 185-186.

Research presented by Paula Forbis on behalf of the Environmental Health Coalition echoed Professor Rabin's findings. The Environmental Health Coalition studied historical local land use decisions in the communities of Barrio Logan, Logan Heights, Sherman Heights, and National City, California, finding that racially discriminatory past land use decisions have current and immediate health impacts. Tr. I-174-181.

More recently, in some (usually larger) cities, Professor Rabin observed that some inequitable conditions (such as substandard housing) have been improved, but only when a court ordered a town to equalize its facilities or blacks became the majority and assumed governance. In either case, improvements occurred only when outside funding was available. By analogy, Professor Rabin concluded that pre-existing conditions adversely impacting health and the environment in low- income and minority communities will only be corrected when substantial outside funding becomes available to these communities. Tr. I-165-169, 185-186.

In addition to highlighting funding issues, stakeholders also focussed on other aspects of EPA's leadership responsibilities. While stakeholders recognized that EPA cannot intrude on local land use decisions, they shared a sense that EPA has not fully explored its opportunities both to address environmental injustices caused by past local land use/zoning decisions and to assist localities in avoiding future injustices.

Recommendation:

The EPA Administrator should exert leadership and become a full partner with local government in eliminating environmental injustice. Specifically, the Administrator should:

1. (In conjunction with other federal agencies) establish a fund to remedy pre-existing environmental injustices in hard-hit low income and minority communities. Tr. I-164-169, 185-186, R. 11.

2. Consider the discriminatory impact of historical land use patterns in deciding whether to use whatever discretionary authority EPA may have to remedy environmental injustices through the state and federal permit process. Tr. I-225-266, III-64.

3. Provide land use guidance for local governments regarding the environmental justice considerations involved in permitting and siting of facilities. Tr. I-184-189, 196, III-47-48.

4. Insist that federally mandated permits to respect local zoning ordinances which protect communities against increases in pollution. (Citizens allege that one such model ordinance in Chester, Pennsylvania was given no weight in the permit process.) Tr. I-74-80.

(Additional recommendations concerning land use/zoning as well as funding are outlined in Section III of this report.)

III. ADDITIONAL POLICY RECOMMENDATIONS.

This section lists all policy recommendations which emerged from the NEJAC meeting (including, for comparison purposes, those identified in Section II). The recommendations cover a wide range of issues, including, in addition to the themes already discussed above, siting criteria, data-gathering for permits, funding, concentrated animal feeding operations, urban air pollution, streamlining/trading/offsets and other alternative compliance schemes, and private sector initiatives.

While many of the general recommendations pertain to tribes among other stakeholders, six recommendations exclusively address the issue of environmental justice for tribal and indigenous peoples. These recommendations are necessary because Indian reservations present unique challenges for applying the principles of environmental justice. As defined by EPA, environmental justice means "The fair treatment and meaningful involvement of all people, regardless of race, color, national origin, or income with respect to the development, implementation, and enforcement of environmental laws, regulations, and policies." The "fair treatment" component of the term means that "no group of people, including racial, ethnic, or socioeconomic group should bear a disproportionate share of the negative environmental consequences resulting from industrial, municipal and commercial operations or the execution of federal, state, local, and tribal programs and policies." [U.S. EPA, Interim Final Guidance for Incorporating Environmental Justice Concerns in EPA's NEPA Compliance Analyses (1997).] This definition includes Indian tribes in two ways. First, tribes are minority groups that can be disadvantaged in socioeconomic terms, and thus tribes are one of the kinds of groups that environmental justice seeks to protect from disproportionate impacts. Second, tribes are also sovereign governments, with the power and responsibility to carry out environmental protection programs. Thus, the challenges of environmental justice for Indian tribes, as outlined by tribal representatives, are two-fold.

First, the communities on Indian reservations tend to fit the definition of environmental justice communities. They are comprised of minority populations and tend to be socially and economically disadvantaged. Indian tribes are diverse, and generalizations should be taken with caution. Many reservation communities have suffered disproportionate impacts to their environments, some of which are the long-term impacts of "development" activities that occurred years or decades ago. Other reservation communities face the prospect of environmental degradation that would result from proposals intended to create jobs and generally improve socioeconomic conditions. Given the rural nature and broad geographic area of many reservations, just to carry the message of environmental justice to the people of reservations is a particular challenge. Communities tend to be far-flung, and the task of outreach when considering a particular environmental permitting issue is difficult at best. Because reservations were established as homelands where tribes could continue to live as separate, self-governing communities, tribal representatives stress that Indian people tend to see themselves as different from other minorities. To the extent that reservation Indians are even aware of the concepts of environmental justice, they may perceive it as something designed to serve the interests of minority groups other than reservation Indians. Many reservations have substantial populations of non-Indians as well as Indians who are members of other tribes. On some reservations, such groups could be considered minorities; on other reservations, the presence of such groups has rendered tribal members minorities within their own homelands.

Second, tribal governments are developing their own environmental programs. Federal environmental laws authorize tribes to operate regulatory programs similar to those administered by the states. The tribal provisions in the federal laws were not enacted, however, until a decade or two after the laws authorizing state programs. The neglect of Indian reservations by Congress in the first generation of federal environmental laws has resulted in less environmental protection infrastructure in Indian country, which can itself be seen as an environmental justice issue. In recent years, many tribes have chosen to establish regulatory programs like those of the states, but they face enormous challenges, in part because tribes generally do not have nonfederal sources of revenue for governmental operations comparable to the states. Tribes also must cope with a confusing body of Supreme Court decisions that opponents of tribal sovereignty can use to challenge tribal programs, and tribes must be prepared to defend against such challenges. Thus, tribes as governments may see environmental justice as another obstacle to the development of effective environmental protection programs. Nevertheless, tribal representatives emphasize that tribes as governments need to understand (1) the legal underpinnings of the principles of environmental justice, and (2) when tribal governments need to apply these principles. Such knowledge, they stress, will take time to develop, and tribes therefore need special consideration from EPA on the underlying issues before being expected to apply the principles of environmental justice as governmental entities. Similarly, much work is still needed on the part of EPA to educate its own staff on the principles of tribal sovereignty and federal Indian law, as well as on the importance of the environment for tribal cultures and philosophies. EPA should therefore proceed with some deliberation and should make extra efforts to ensure that tribes are well informed on the basic environmental laws and environmental justice principles prior to entering into discussions about permits in Indian country.

Unless otherwise indicated, each of the following eighty (80) recommendations is addressed to EPA.

Reframing or expanding the nature of the inquiry:

1. Reword EPA's inquiry as follows:

   In order to secure protection from environmental degradation for all citizens, *what factors should be determinative* when a federal permitting authority (or state or local agency with delegated permitting responsibilities) makes a decision regarding a new pollution-generating facility proposing to operate in a minority and/or low-income community that already has a number of such facilities? Tr. I-235.

2. Reconvene the Interagency Task Force on Environmental Justice because environmental permitting involves a broader range of agencies than EPA (e.g., the Department of Defense, Department of Energy, Army Corps of Engineers, Bureau of Indian Affairs). Tr. I-297-327, III-223-225.

3. Address permits issued by state, regional, and local agencies as well as those required under federal law. Tr. I-64-65.

4. Ensure broader representation of environmental justice populations and community organizations on federal advisory committees, especially those developing guidelines to be applied in permits. Tr. I-214.

5. Ensure that each relevant regulatory and permitting office, at EPA and in other federal agencies, has a diverse work force. Tr. I-214-216.

Legal factors

6. Find legal authority to address the potential effects of long-term exposure to multiple low-level toxins in permits issued in environmental justice communities in Principle 15 of the Rio Declaration on the Environment and Development. Tr. I-239-240 (and attached prepared statement).

7. Find legal authority to address environmental justice concerns in permitting in the International Convention on the Elimination of All Forms of Racial Discrimination, ratified by the United States in 1994 and made applicable to executive agencies, including EPA, by Executive Order 13107. Tr. I-239-240 (and attached prepared statement).

8. Find legal authority to address environmental justice concerns in permitting in the National Environmental Policy Act (NEPA). Tr. I-170-171.

9. In the alternative, since NEPA provides the best mechanism for ensuring wide-ranging consideration of needs, impacts, and alternatives, voluntarily subject more EPA permits to the NEPA process, utilizing the CEQ guidelines for cumulative impact review in the environmental justice context. Tr. I-170-171.

10. Find legal authority to address environmental justice concerns in permitting in the general provisions of the Clean Air Act. Tr. I-46-59, 237-240 (and attachments).

11. Find legal authority to address environmental justice concerns about cumulative burdens and their associated health risks in permits issued in urban areas in section 112(k) of the Clean Air Act, 42 U.S.C. 7412(k). Tr. I-293-296.

12. Find legal authority to address environmental justice concerns in permits issued under the Clean Water Act. Tr. I-46-59, 237-240 (and attachments).

13. Find legal authority to address environmental justice concerns in permits issued under the Resource Conservation and Recovery Act. Tr. I-46-59, 237-240 (and attachments).

14. Find legal authority to address environmental justice concerns in permits issued under the Safe Drinking Water, Toxic Substances Control, and Federal Insecticide, Fungicide, and Rodenticide Acts. Tr. I-46-59, 237-240 (and attachments).

15. Finally, make environmental justice criteria applicable to permitting through rulemaking so as to bind states and also protect them from suits alleging that they are arbitrary and capricious when they deny a permit on environmental justice grounds. Tr. I-204-208, 285-287.

Substantive permit criteria:

16. Address the following factors as bases for denying permits: (1) negative health risks; (2) racially disproportionate burdens; (3) cumulative and synergistic adverse impacts on human health and the environment; (4) high aggregation of risk from multiple sources; (5) community vulnerability based on the number of children, elderly, or asthmatics; (6) cultural practices, including Tribal and indigenous cultures and cultural reliance on land and water that may become pathways of toxic exposure;

and (7) proximity to residential areas and adequacy of buffer zones. Tr. I-45-46, 74-80, 195, 225-227, 234-237, 240-246, 250-251, 268, 271-272, 281-282, 293-296, 301, 318, III-20-23, 77-83, R. 13, 20.

17. Explore using both a substantive alternatives analysis and a rigid sequencing approach for permitting in highly impacted communities. Begin with an alternatives analysis. Deny a permit if there is a practicable alternative to siting the facility in or near an impacted community and use regulatory incentives to facilitate permitting at the alternative site (e.g., expedited permitting, emission trades, alternative compliance requirements such as emission caps and budgets, etc.). If a facility must be sited in a highly impacted community, strive to avoid adverse impacts; then minimize adverse impacts that cannot be avoided (e.g., through specialized control technology, alternative production processes, site-specific land management practices, buffer zones, alternative traffic routes, etc.); finally, provide compensatory mitigation (such as reducing emissions from other sources in the area) for the remaining risks. Similar approaches can be found in the Clean Water Act section 404 permit program, the Endangered Species incidental takings permit program, and transferable development rights used to protect historic buildings. Tr. I-228-229 and attachment.[2]

18. In addition to cumulative exposure, consider: (1) health and ecological risk assessments; (2) the economic burden of medical costs and lost productivity; (3) access to health care; (4) psychological impacts; (5) the risk of chemical accidents; (6) emergency preparedness; (7) community right-to-know in permitting; and (7) an applicant's compliance history in issuing permits in low-income and minority communities. Tr. I-224-227, III-50-59, 84-85.

19. Recognize that a community's environmental concerns may be considerably broader than the media-specific technical criteria used by federal and state permit agencies. Indeed, community concerns encompass such quality-of-life issues as: (1) noise; (2) dust; (3) constant truck traffic; (4) roadway congestion; (5) blocked roadway access due to truck parking violations; (6) debris falling from trash trucks; (7) safety issues raised by trucks speeding through residential areas; (8) rats; (9) odors; (10) house vibrations; (11) sleep deprivation due to all-night traffic; (12) deteriorated property values; and (13) general neighborhood decline. EPA should clarify that federally required permits need to consider such affronts, because states administering delegated permit programs have told adjacent communities that permit writers lack jurisdiction over such problems. Tr. I-68-72, 224-227, 360-361.

20. Use health-based statistics to identify geographic areas that need to be treated more cautiously for permitting purposes; work in and around Philadelphia provides a model for such an approach. Tr. III-38-39, 53-54, 84.

21. Consider the level of franchise (i.e., access to, and ability to influence, government) of different communities in permitting and establish more preventative approaches where necessary to protect the integrity of the permit process. Tr. III-58-59. (This recommendation stems from the fact that low-income and minority communities historically have lacked the resources necessary to monitor polluting facilities in their communities and, if violations are found, either to persuade government

---

[2] A letter dated April 18, 2000 from Eileen Gauna to NEJAC outlines this approach in more detail.

officials to take enforcement action or to bring their own citizen enforcement actions.) Tr. I-45-46.

22. Require federally mandated permits to respect local zoning ordinances which protect communities against increases in pollution; citizens allege that one such model ordinance in Chester, Pennsylvania was given no weight in the permit process. Tr. I-74-80.

23. Consider the discriminatory impact of historical land use patterns in deciding whether to use whatever discretionary authority EPA may have to remedy environmental injustices through the state and federal permit process. Tr. I-225-266, III-64.

24. Require an allocation mechanism that addresses *future* projects so that the first permit applicant does not absorb all of a neighborhood's potential for growth (e.g., traffic capacity or clean air increment). Tr. I-226, R. 11.

25. Take cognizance of whether permit applicants propose to displace older, more polluting facilities. Tr. I-169-170.

26. Expedite the permit process for facilities that have been invited into communities and enjoy widespread community support since speed and predictability offer important market advantages to permit applicants. Tr. I-171-174, R. 12.

27. Focus more attention on pollution prevention activities, both as a condition of permits and as a way to avoid toxic releases altogether. Tr. I-195-196.

Siting criteria and land use:

28. Adhere to the recommendations of NEJAC's Waste and Facility Siting Subcommittee as currently being detailed in a draft brochure entitled "Social Aspects of Siting RCRA Hazardous Waste Facilities." Tr. I-210-211, III-46-47.

29. Adhere to the recommendations of NEJAC's Waste and Facility Siting Subcommittee as detailed in their report and related resolution on waste transfer stations.[3] The report outlines the need for best management practice manuals for both facility siting and operations. In addition, the report calls for siting criteria, a planning process to assure a more equitable distribution of facilities, design and operating practice requirements, potential emission reduction requirements, increased community participation, and enhanced enforcement, among other measures. The report reflects a two (2)-year study of transfer stations demonstrating that, absent a federal baseline, there is enormous variability in the operating practices of waste transfer stations and strong community dissatisfaction, particularly where facilities were clustered as they are in New York City and Washington, D.C. Tr. III-143-152. (A copy of the Subcommittee's report and resolution can be found in the NEJAC Executive Summary Report on the EPA Web Site as Appendix B. For additional discussion of the problems associated with waste transfer stations, see Tr. I-33-34, 189-190.)

---

[3] Waste transfer stations are facilities where municipal waste is unloaded from collection vehicles and subsequently re-loaded onto larger transport vehicles to be taken to a disposal site. Waste transfer stations allow communities to move waste economically over long distances.

30. Provide land use guidance for local governments regarding the environmental justice considerations involved in permitting and siting of facilities. Tr. I-184-189, 196, III-47-48, R. 12.

Public participation and community involvement:

31. Direct the Inspector General to conduct a full audit of the State of Louisiana permitting programs with particular attention to violations of EPA public participation regulations, NEJAC's public participation guidelines, and the U.S. Constitution. Tr. I-284, 344-358, 360-362, III-189-198. (A copy of the Resolution adopted by NEJAC can be found in the NEJAC Executive Summary Report on the EPA Web Site as Appendix B.) See also Tr. I-82.

32. (From the Council on Environmental Quality), convene community-level interagency meetings modelled on successful meetings in Los Angeles and New York City. The meetings would serve to apply principles of environmental justice at the community level, generate a mutually agreed upon agenda, and spotlight local environmental justice problems. Participants should include community leaders, government officials, and Congressional representatives. The meeting should endeavor to produce a series of commitments to the local community. Tr. I-29-37. (While the agenda at such a meeting probably would range well beyond permitting, the meeting could provide a forum to resolve permit issues, among other community concerns.)

33. Adopt binding public participation requirements which ensure permit writers will consult with affected communities "early and often." Tr. I-87-88, 91-99, 129-130, 198-199, R. 14-16, 19-20. Specifically:

   a. Contact potentially affected communities as soon as an agency is aware that a permit application <u>may</u> be filed or that emissions from a facility <u>may</u> increase, but in no event later than immediately upon receipt of the permit application or notice that emissions could increase. Tr. I-91-92, 129-130, 132-133, 198-199, 272, 279, R. 19.
   b. Hold an initial hearing or informal meeting with the potentially affected communities immediately upon receipt of a permit application. R. 14-16, 19-22.
   c. Accurately identify community leaders; do not rely on local government to represent low-income or minority communities. Tr. I-129-130.
   d. Develop a plan for community involvement in conjunction with the community. Tr. I-91-92.
   e. Require a community outreach plan modelled on those used with success in the brownfields grants program; follow up to ensure that the plan is implemented. Tr. I-131-132, R. 12.
   f. Use broadcast media and other effective forms of communication to advertise the public participation process. Tr. I-94-95, R. 19.
   g. Require permit notices in newspapers to be printed in legible print and to be placed in spots likely to attract the attention of potentially affected residents. Tr. I-82-83, 355, R. 14.
   h. In public notices of proposed permits, describe what the discharge/emission means to the community in lay, rather than technical, terms. Otherwise,

comment periods end before communities learn about potential impacts. Tr. I-87-88, 101-103, 132-133, III-20, R. 14.

    i. Utilize local government resources as well by bringing local government into the process as early as possible. Tr. I-95-97, 187-189.

    j. Make technical reports accessible to the community as soon as they are available, rather than holding them internally until commencement of a 30-day comment period. The 30-day comment period is often an inadequate time in which to obtain independent technical advice on the complicated issues involved in permitting. (Presumably, this recommendation would require agencies to establish a publicly accessible permit docket.) Tr. I-132-133, 274-275, R. 14.

    k. Extend the 30-day public comment period for complicated permits. Tr. I-132-135.

34. Adopt permit conditions which provide communities with adequate test data and sufficient control over ongoing monitoring to ensure the safe operation of a facility. Tr. I-45-46, 202. In pre-meeting interviews, stakeholders identified a variety of obvious, as well as innovative, ways to accomplish this objective, including:

    a. bucket brigades in which citizens learn how to collect and send samples to EPA-approved labs (used as the basis for at least one successful enforcement action in Region IX),

    b. requiring companies with continuous emission monitoring to have digital printouts on stacks reporting their emission limits,

    c. Community Advisory Committees,

    d. monitoring and enforcement by other governmental entities (e.g., tribes and local governments),

    e. use of qualified consultants,

    f. community-facility good neighbor agreements, and

    g. daily posting of compliance data on the web. R. 22-23.

35. Assess, for the purposes of developing benchmarks, whether required public participation programs associated with permitting are working effectively because there is considerable testimony to the effect that such efforts are extremely problematic. Tr. III-132-133.

36. Make qualified, independent experts available to the local community to review permit technicalities. Tr. I-101.

37. Require permit applicants to certify under penalty of perjury that the information they provide to the public is complete and accurate. Tr. I-133-134.

38. Provide training for citizens and tribal governments on the permitting process itself. Tr. I-101, 210-211, 365-366, III-20-21.

39. Develop a citizens' guide to grandfathered facilities to facilitate citizen monitoring and involvement in permit reissuance for these facilities. Tr. III-115-116.

40. Identify existing legal authority to address cumulative impacts in permitting; make a list of these authorities available to environmental justice communities. Tr. III-116.

41. Require permit applicants to make geographic information system ("GIS"), demographic, and other computerized data (including the computers to review the data) available to local communities. Tr. I-191-194.

42. Address, through permits, communication networks extending from the community to the upper echelons of EPA in the event of chemical accidents or explosions. Tr. III-59-60.

Data gathering for permits:

43. (To EPA and other agencies), recognize the excellent health effects research now being done by community organizations and support further community-driven (i.e., community controlled) health effects research to ensure better permitting decisions. Tr. III-55-56.

44. (To ATSDR), incorporate more communities of color in research, such as the recent report on the economic burden of medical costs and lost productivity, since such information is relevant to permitting. Tr. III-84-85.

Funding:

45. (To EPA, in conjunction with other federal agencies), establish a fund to remedy pre-existing environmental injustices in hard-hit low income and minority communities. Such a fund is an essential precondition to improved permitting. Tr. I-164-169, 185-186, R. 11.

46. (To EPA as well as to the National Institute for Environmental Health Sciences, Agency for Toxic Substance Disease Registry, the National Institutes of Health, Center for Disease Control, and other agencies with health responsibilities), fund research on cumulative exposure analysis analogous to the research conducted by Communities for a Better Environment along the Aladema Corridor in Los Angeles. There, researchers used GIS mapping systems, demographic data, the Toxic Release Inventory database, other facility siting information, and a physical inventory conducted by community members to publish a report on cumulative exposure entitled "Holding Our Breath." Noteworthy findings included the fact that 70% of area facilities were not reporting to environmental agencies and, hence, were not identified in agency databases. In addition, an industrial chrome plating facility had been permitted immediately adjacent to an elementary school. Such research can be an essential tool for community empowerment, enabling communities to identify appropriate permit terms and conditions or circumstances in which permitting should not go forward. (The Los Angeles research was funded by the National Institute of Environmental Health Sciences, UCLA School of Public Health, Center for Occupational Environmental Health, Labor Occupation Safety and Health Divisions, and the USC Southern California Environmental Health Science Center.) Tr. I-60-65.

47. Attach environmental health funds to permits, with special emphasis on communities of color, children, women, and elders. Tr. I-203, III-59.

48. Provide funds for universities to provide independent technical advice on permitting issues to affected communities. Tr. I-134, 215-216.

49. Make funding available to states to engage in activities related to improved permitting in environmental justice communities, including site and community data-gathering and evaluation, expanded public participation, and community training. Tr. I-207.

50. Make funding available to encourage youth in low-income and minority communities to pursue environmental careers so that permit agencies can employ a diverse workforce. Tr. I-214-216.

51. Recognize the special funding needs of tribes to develop regulatory and permitting infrastructure. Tr. I-241-245.

Enforcement of permits and related regulatory requirements:

52. Ensure that EPA guidance on environmental justice reaches beyond the headquarters level to each of the regional offices and, in particular, regional permit writers. Tr. I-155-160, 277.

53. Ensure that EPA guidance on environmental justice reaches beyond to state personnel, especially permit writers, administering federally approved or required programs. Tr. I-160.

54. Assess all delegated state permit programs for compliance with federal legal requirements and withdraw federal program delegation in states which fail to implement the requirements. Tr. I-84, 102.

55. Address unpermitted or underpermitted activity, since this is a major problem. (For example, NEJAC heard testimony that a facility in Arizona is being allowed to operate even though EPA Region IX believes that the facility does not have an effective permit.) Tr. I- 144, III-62-63.

56. (To EPA and States), use enforcement programs to capture the economic benefits of permit violations so that corporations cannot profit from pollution. (See the NEJAC Enforcement Subcommittee's resolution and report on "Credible Deterrence," can be found in the NEJAC Executive Summary Report on the EPA Web Site as Appendix B.) Tr. III-164-165.

57. Be more assertive in exercising regulatory authority to reopen permits for grandfathered facilities, many of which would not have been approved under modern standards. One stakeholder asserted that, under modern "takings" case law, old polluting facilities can be shut down where there is a documented technical basis that they are causing an adverse impact. Tr. I-169-170.

58. Explore an initiative to clean up 1,712 high priority RCRA facilities. Tr. III-47.

59. Conduct a pilot test of enforcement options against waste transfer stations in New York City. Tr. III-152-153.

60. Adhere to the NEJAC Enforcement Subcommittee's resolution recommending that EPA refrain from recognizing state and local authority to grant variances from federally mandated air pollution permit requirements in cases of alleged malfunction, start-up, shut down, and maintenance. The Subcommittee cautioned

that, in practice, state and local variances receive little scrutiny, reflect highly subjective standards, and are relatively easy to obtain. Federal recognition of these variances would preclude both federal and community enforcement suits, potentially increasing emissions in low-income and minority communities which disproportionately host polluting facilities. Instead, the Subcommittee recommended that EPA exercise case-by-case prosecutorial discretion to determine whether or not Clean Air Act violations due to alleged malfunction, start-up, shut down, or maintenance merit enforcement. (A copy of the Subcommittee's resolution can be found in the NEJAC Executive Summary Report on the EPA Web Site as Appendix B.) Tr. III-164.

Concentrated animal feeding operations:

61. Accelerate the schedule for permitting concentrated animal feeding operations because now there is virtually a complete lack of permitting and a tremendous need for enforcement. Tr. III-25-26, 129-131, 178-180.

62. Require states to assume responsibility for permitting concentrated animal feeding operations within their jurisdiction. (A corollary recommendation is to educate states that have not had much experience with concentrated animal feeding operations about the associated environmental problems, because states often assume that these facilities do not discharge and, hence, do not require permits.) Where states are not interested in permitting these facilities, conduct federal inspections. Tr. III-130-131.

63. Investigate compliance with permit and regulatory requirements in Oklahoma where there has been a rapid proliferation of concentrated animal feeding operations in a small geographic area. Tr. I- 332-344, III-131-132, 180. (See related resolutions pertaining to tribal land, below.)

Urban air pollution:

64. Adhere to the recommendations of the NEJAC Air and Water Subcommittee on the urban air toxics strategy. (See their report, a copy of which can be found as Appendix C on the EPA Web Site.) Many of these recommendations address significant outstanding issues, such as choice of pollutants, selection of monitoring location and technology -- issues which remain relevant during the implementation phase of the strategy. Tr. III-116-120.

65. Structure public hearings and workshops around the country on implementation of the urban air toxics strategy to address monitoring questions, choice of technology, and state and local pilot projects. Tr. III-116-120.

66. Develop model materials on urban air toxics so that when state and local governments start implementing the program, communities can participate effectively. Tr. III-120-121.

67. Address the environmental justice implications of energy generation. Tr. III-119-127.

68. Address the environmental justice implications of Tier II reductions in the amount of sulfur in commercially sold gasoline. The concern is that, as refineries tighten

production processes to produce cleaner fuels, they will emit more locally. Trading programs may allow facilities to offset local emission increases with estimates of emission reductions from cleaner fuels. Tr. III-127-129.

69. Create a two (2)-page document informing communities impacted by Tier II-related local emission increases how to ensure new source review of plant process changes and reasonable reductions in local emissions. Tr. III-127-129.

70. Assess the pollution effects of permitted and proposed nuclear incinerators such as that proposed for Idaho Falls. Tr. III-134.

71. Take specific actions with respect to Puerto Rico's state implementation plan (SIP); namely, a) require Puerto Rico to revise the SIP because the regulations for power plants do not include federally mandated emission limitations on sulfur dioxide and particulates, even in nonattainment areas, b) require these power plants to use clean fuel (i.e., sulfur content of no more than 0.5%), and c) require these power plants to install continuous emission monitoring for sulfur dioxide. Tr. III-135-143, 183.

72. In consultation with the U.S. Department of Transportation, convene a meeting of the New Jersey Department of Transportation, the New Jersey Department of Environmental Protection, and the South Jersey Transportation Authority to address: a) long-term air quality issues associated with the Atlantic City Tunnel Project, b) community exposure to contaminated soil during construction, c) potential post-construction impacts such as flooding and safety, and d) the broader policy issues implicated by this project. Tr. III-153-155. (A copy of the NEJAC Resolution can be found in the NEJAC Executive Summary Report on the EPA Web Site as Appendix B.)

Streamlining, trading, offsets and other alternative compliance schemes:

73. Five different recommendations for "alternative compliance schemes" emerged; some of these are mutually exclusive:

   a) (From EPA's Air Program), explore whether, in certain communities heavily burdened by toxics or large concentrations of pollutants, the desire for economic development can be harnessed to drive reduced total loadings of toxics. Specifically, communities could proactively undertake toxic reductions (e.g., replace diesel-fueled buses with natural gas-fueled vehicles, retrofit pollution controls on existing trucks and buses, replace oil-based solvents with water-based products) and identify still further potential emission reductions. Accomplished emission reductions would provide room for new growth; targeted, desired reductions would identify potential offsets for new sources. Both types of reductions -- and the streamlined, expedited permitting EPA would offer new sources in these communities -- would make the communities more attractive to new development than communities where further growth would cause environmental justice problems. Tr. I-140-148, III-25, 29-46.

   b) Explore whether global facility permits, used in several states, provide an opportunity to reduce total emission loadings. Tr. III-39.

   c) Recognize that compliance alternatives are a huge potential loophole in permitting. Trading, in particular, allows a company to bypass public

31

involvement and obviate community gains in permitting. EPA, therefore, should adhere to the recommendations of the Enforcement Subcommittee of NEJAC as outlined in their comments on the Economic Incentive Program document, a copy of which can be found in the NEJAC Executive Summary Report on the EPA Web Site as Appendix B. Tr. I-145-148, 318, 327-332, III-62-64, 167-178.

   d) If trading is to be allowed, consider some or all of the following limitations on it:

   - restrict its use to situations that directly and favorably impact conditions in environmental justice communities. Tr. III-113-114.
   - avoid using counties as a geographic area for emission trading purposes because California has counties (like San Bernadino) that are as big as Connecticut, Rhode Island, and Massachusetts combined. Reducing pollution in the county as a whole may still impact environmental justice communities adversely or disproportionately. Tr. III-41-45.
   - avoid emission trading of lead emissions. Tr. III-163.
   - consider that less poisoning of a community is still poisoning. Tr. I-271-272, III-59.
   - prohibit streamlining or expediting the permit process in overly impacted communities because additional time may be needed to evaluate the additional complex issues presented in these communities. Tr. I-227-228.

   e) Create an environmental emission trading review board of representatives of environmental justice communities; federal, state, and local officials; and experts in health, engineering, and real estate. The board would rank and prioritize environmental justice projects, contract for professional services where necessary, use a pre-funded $50 million emission trading bank to address disparate impacts, and auction emission reduction credits. Tr. I-230-234.

Tribal and Indigenous Peoples:

74. Recognize that EPA has a special legal relationship with tribes who are sovereign governments. In recognition of that relationship, educate representatives of both regulated communities (e.g., industry) and regulators (i.e., state and federal government agencies) on indigenous cultural values. Lack of understanding of indigenous cultural, religious, and historical values permeates permitting on or adjacent to tribal lands. Tr. I-240-246, III-20-23, 77-83.

75. Notify potentially affected tribal governments and members directly of pending review of permits as soon as a permit application is submitted. Tr. I-245, III-20. Identify community leaders accurately; do not rely on local government to represent environmental justice communities, because many low-income and/or minority communities do not have visibility or political influence. Tr. 1-129-130. However, consistent with the government-to-government relationship with tribal governments and the federal trust responsibility owed to them, in the case of Native American communities, initial outreach efforts should, in the first instance, be directed to the tribal governments as representatives of their communities and to their tribal members. Additional outreach to other potentially affected persons and nongovernmental organizations also may be needed to ensure optimal public participation.

76. Encourage and support ongoing consultation between tribes and the permitting agency throughout the permit process. Tr. I-242-245, III-20.

77. Modify public participation requirements to account for the special problems attendant in reaching small, isolated rural communities on tribal lands. Tr. I-86-88.

78. Develop core water quality standards for permitting on tribal lands lacking such standards. Federal action is necessary because tribes which have adopted their own standards have found those standards attacked approved water quality standards, protect the quality of reservation waters from excessive degradation due to licensing or permitting activities by developing, in consultation and agreement with tribes, core water quality standards. Tr. I-127-128.

79. Include tribal lands in best management practice and regulatory requirements applicable to waste transfer stations. Tr. I-127-128.

(Note related recommendations #16, pertaining to substantive permit criteria, #38, pertaining to training, #51, pertaining to funding, and #63 pertaining to concentrated animal feeding operations on tribal land.)

Private sector initiatives:

80. Encourage the private sector to address environmental justice issues. Specific initiatives suggested by industry representatives for the private sector include:

    • Utilize the NEJAC guidelines on public participation. Tr. I-198-199.

    • Commit to listen, record, and respond to every question asked of a permit applicant at a public meeting. Tr. I-198-199, R. 20.

    • Change corporate policies on siting and acquisition so that environmental personnel are integrated into decision-making earlier in the process, before companies are heavily invested in a particular site. (Under current practice, siting is primarily market-driven. Only after a lengthy analysis of non-environmental factors, such as access to supplies and transportation corridors, growth potential, etc., does a company look at the community, its environment and quality of life.) R. 12.

IV. APPENDICES (On EPA Web Site)

A – Pre-Meeting Report
        http://www.epa.gov/oeca/main/ej/nejacpub.html

B – December 1999 NEJAC Executive Council Meeting
        http://www.epa.gov/oeca/main/ej/nejac/past_nmeet.html

C – Air/Water Subcommittee Comments on Draft Urban Air Strategy
        http://www.epa.gov/oeca/main/ej/nejacpub.html

D – Transcripts from November 30-December 2, 1999 NEJAC Meeting
    I – November 30, 1999, Plenary Session w/Permitting Public Comment
        Session
    II – December 1, 1999, General Public Comment Period
    III – December 2, 1999, Plenary Session
        http://www.epa.gov/oeca/main/ej/nejacpub.html

PRE-MEETING REPORT: ENVIRONMENTAL JUSTICE IN THE PERMITTING PROCESS

A Report on Stakeholders' Views

APPENDIX A of the Final Report "Environmental Justice in The Permitting Process - EPA 300-R-00-004

Prepared for the National Environmental Justice Advisory Council
A Federal Advisory Committee to the
U.S. Environmental Protection Agency

Frances A. Dubrowski
University of Maryland School of Public Affairs
Consultant

TABLE OF CONTENTS

EXECUTIVE SUMMARY

Environmental permitting poses a true challenge to the Environmental Protection Agency(EPA). EPA's mission is to ensure, among other things, that all Americans, regardless of race, color, national origin or economic status, are protected from significant risks to human health and the natural environment -- air, water, and land -- where they live, learn and work. EPA must carry out this mission consistent with Executive Order 12898 on environmental justice and federal environmental laws.

Environmental permitting represents the principal arena where companies and communities confront each other over the details of which businesses may operate, where, and under what conditions in or near residential neighborhoods. In short, it is where the rubber hits the road in terms of implementing a host of regulatory standards designed, with varying degrees of adequacy, to protect health and the environment.

This report presents the results of interviews about the permit process with twenty (20) stakeholders drawn from government (EPA, Tribal, State, or local), industry, academia, and community organizations. These discussions revealed common concerns -- and fundamental disagreements -- over where and how to integrate environmental justice in the permitting process.

All stakeholders agreed that EPA needs to address the issue of incorporating environmental justice considerations in permitting because communities increasingly are insisting upon a broader view of permitting and because neither companies nor permit writers know what is expected of them. While several stakeholders stressed that permitting is only one of several contexts in which government agencies need to respond to environmental justice concerns, all agreed that permitting guidelines are a high priority.

Stakeholders differed as to what the Agency's permitting goal should be. Tribal, State, local government, academic and community stakeholders thought agencies should address pre-existing conditions with potential health and environmental impacts. EPA stakeholders, in general, agreed, though several expressed an interest in doing so only for a limited category of permits. Industry stakeholders acknowledged the need to deal with cumulative risk in some fashion (though not necessarily in permitting), and expressed a willingness to explore approaches. Stakeholders identified twelve (12) government or private sector approaches to addressing environmental justice.

Stakeholders also agreed that the current permit process typically does not address environmental justice issues, though they differed as to what transpires.

Industry stakeholders saw the process as largely centered on technical issues of compliance; government stakeholders saw themselves addressing a broader set of issues; community stakeholders saw the process as driven towards finding a means to grant the applicant a permit.

Stakeholders identified numerous problems with the current permit program, including failure to consider environmental justice or cumulative impacts, lack of clear guidance for permit writers on how to address environmental justice, and lack of adequate public participation.

Non-Agency stakeholders agreed that the current program does not adequately include community input, while EPA stakeholders held a range of opinions on this subject, ranking the Agency's performance anywhere from "poor" to quite successful. Stakeholders held mixed views on the utility of Alternative Dispute Resolution as a tool for facilitating stakeholder cooperation.

Stakeholders recommended: (1) expanded public involvement in permitting; (2) addressing cumulative impacts (in permitting or elsewhere); and (3) clarifying what the permit writer should consider and how the permit writer should react when confronted with a disparate impact. Many suggested the need for legal guidance -- presumably from the Office of General Counsel -- in this area. Stakeholders also acknowledged opportunities for mutual industry/community gain in permitting.

Community, Tribal, State, local government, and academic stakeholders enthusiastically endorsed community monitoring of facility compliance. Industry stakeholders were willing to entertain proposals for community monitoring, but expressed caution about data adequacy and accuracy. EPA officials generally were skeptical of the extent to which community monitoring assists technical compliance, but might be less skeptical of its value for enhancing community-facility relations. Stakeholders also identified additional areas of inquiry into environmental justice issues.

PURPOSE

EPA, through the Office of Environmental Justice, has asked the National Environmental Justice Advisory Council (NEJAC) to provide advice and recommendations on the following question:

In order to secure protection from environmental degradation for all citizens, what factors should be considered by a federal permitting authority, as well as state or local agencies with delegated permitting responsibilities, in the decision-making process prior to allowing a new pollution-generating facility to operate in a minority and/or low-income community that may already have a number of such facilities?

To address this question, NEJAC has scheduled a three-day public meeting of industry, government (federal, Tribal, State, and local), academic, and community stakeholders to explore whether and how the issue of environmental justice could be integrated into the permitting process. The discussion is a prelude to a comprehensive report addressing stakeholder perspectives on this significant issue as well as recommendations for Agency review.

This report summarizes interviews with a representative sampling of stakeholders scheduled to participate in the upcoming public meeting. By interviewing a diverse group of stakeholders in advance, the Office of Environmental Justice intends to lay the groundwork for a focused and productive policy dialogue, make efficient use of the time and talents of participating stakeholders, and ensure that any advice and recommendations for Agency action reflect careful attention to the concerns of all affected parties. This report, therefore, aims to capture the views and voices of the stakeholders in their own words, identifying both potential areas of agreement as well as fundamental differences in perspective.

METHODOLOGY

Twenty (20) stakeholders were interviewed for this report: eight (8) representing EPA programs, three (3) representing industrial interests, three (3) representing academia, three (3) representing State or local governments, two (2) representing community organizations, and one (1) representing a Native American Tribe. A list of the stakeholders and their organizational affiliations is attached as Attachment 1.

Each stakeholder was asked a series of questions (Attachment 2). In addition, the stakeholders were invited to deviate from the questions to discuss issues, concerns, or insights triggered by the questions and also to suggest other appropriate areas of inquiry.

This methodology has both inherent strengths and weaknesses. The relatively small sample size made it possible to conduct in-depth interviews, focusing not just on stakeholder opinions, but also on the reasoning behind those opinions. On the other hand, the small number of stakeholders and their relative distribution (EPA vs. non-EPA representatives) precludes any quantitative analysis of the results. This report, therefore, presents the results of these interviews principally in terms of their content, adding only the most obvious quantitative references (e.g., where "all," "many," "most," or "several" stakeholders expressed a particular view).

RESULTS

1. The importance of environmental justice in permitting.

All stakeholders agreed that EPA needs to address the issue of incorporating environmental justice considerations into the permitting process and decisions. They differed only in the strength with which they held these views. Even the mildest response acknowledged that *"we need to work out the role of environmental justice in the permitting process."* Most stakeholders ranked the issue as *"important"* to *"extremely important."*

Several stakeholders stressed that permitting is only one of several contexts in which government agencies need to respond to environmental justice concerns. As one put it, *"Environmental justice is much more than permitting.*

Doing a good job on the front end makes permitting go much better." This State stakeholder stressed the need to incorporate environmental justice concerns into agency policies, programs, standards, and enforcement procedures as well as permits. An industry stakeholder, citing numerous types of government decisions with environmental justice impacts, echoed the sentiment, *"Permitting has a role, but it's not a one-stop answer to environmental justice.... We don't want the permit program to be viewed as the sole fix to 200 years of social ills."*

On the other hand, stakeholders seemed to acknowledge the importance of placing a high priority on tackling permit concerns immediately. One stakeholder emphasized the confusion, confrontation, and delay that will occur until EPA resolves how to handle environmental justice in permitting. Another emphasized the opportunity to avoid end-of-process Title VI and community complaints. Another concluded, *"Permitting is forward-looking."* A third noted permitting is a *"promising place to address the problem.... Permits respond to local conditions as compared to a one-size-fits-all national approach."* One summarized community perspectives, stating that: *"Permitting is the gateway for emissions and the first in a series of possible events that could lead to noncompliance and contamination. Minimum standards are supposed to ensure safety (or so people assume), but in the end, it is the host community that bears the risk. Standards, policies, programs are important, but communities often don't have the resources to participate at that level. So for them, permitting is the key."*

While acknowledging the need to address environmental justice, stakeholders candidly shared their uncertainty about how to proceed. As one put it, *"This is not something we have thought about until recently."* Another observed, *"EPA and States are still on a learning curve about how to handle environmental justice issues."* Still another, raising similar questions, recognized that addressing the issue could *"potentially represent a sea change in the way we do permitting."*

This dichotomy between a clear goal and an uncertain implementation mechanism frustrates Agency officials. On the one hand, EPA, State, and local government stakeholders expressed a sincere desire to address environmental justice. Typical comments included the following: *"We are committed to look at [environmental justice in permitting] and seek opportunities for meaningful progress;" "We want to make sure all communities are involved, including environmental justice communities, ... and our decisions occur in as open a process as possible;"* and *"We can't do a proper permit without looking at those [environmental justice] concerns."*

On the other hand, despite their intentions, Agency officials admitted they can show little practical real world impact to environmental justice communities. An EPA official confessed, *"There is a real bafflement on the part of states and EPA as to how to take environmental justice into account. We don't have the statutory authority, expertise, or tools. We pass around stories and articles and realize we have to do more, but we're not sure what."* A State stakeholder explained: *"Permit writers lack an objective standard or protocol to accept or reject a project. There is no federal definition of disparate impact, so we feel open to suit."* This stakeholder urged EPA to provide the leadership: *"We are looking to EPA for the tools on how to do this."* An EPA official, in turn, said *"Good question ... this is the guidance we want to get from NEJAC."*

2.   NEJAC as a forum for addressing this issue.

One key question interviews sought to determine was: Is NEJAC the appropriate forum for initiating a dialogue on this issue? While a few stakeholders demurred on this question (due to lack of direct working experience with NEJAC), all of the stakeholders familiar with NEJAC agreed that NEJAC is, or could be, an appropriate forum for this exercise. Within this overall umbrella of approval, however, stakeholder perception of NEJAC varied, as outlined below.

NEJAC won very high marks from many stakeholders representing community organizations, state and local government, and academia. One stakeholder explained: *"NEJAC is one of the few bureaucratic institutions where community organizations feel they can come and speak openly."* A community representative echoed the sentiment, *"No one else is even trying"* to address these issues. Another stated, *"NEJAC has been very important in lifting up questions about environmental and economic justice."* Academic stakeholders also praised the Council, *"NEJAC can be a very useful forum. It provides the Agency with a place to have interested stakeholders ventilate their concerns. The Agency has used it historically as a good source of information."* Another added, *"They are as good as any forum -- as good as we have.... They do a good job within the limits they have."*

By contrast, NEJAC earned more measured acceptance and respect from industry stakeholders. *(E.g., "I don't see why they wouldn't be a good forum [to address this issue]. The alternatives are not obviously superior.")*

Within EPA itself, reaction to NEJAC was considerably more mixed. Some Agency officials rated the Council quite highly. One described NEJAC as *"the most knowledgeable about environmental justice issues and concerns."* Several answered simply, *"I can't think of any group who would be better at bringing the right folks together. If not NEJAC, then who?"* Others had had little contact with NEJAC or expressed confusion about how to utilize NEJAC output in program decision-making. *E.g., "NEJAC is a good forum to bounce ideas off, get input from, and share ideas and learning with, but ... one downside of NEJAC is that its various committees are not taking an integrated look at overlapping committee issues. So it is hard to figure out their hierarchy of objectives given limited resources -- in other words, how to make it all fit together at the end of the day. But NEJAC can give valuable feedback on this."* Several flatly stated that NEJAC did not sufficiently reflect pressure from industry, Congress, and the states to make meaningful recommendations for Agency action. (E.g., *"The question is broader than NEJAC"*).

Roughly half of the stakeholders cautioned that, even if NEJAC addresses this issue, there is a need to look beyond NEJAC to a broader group of stakeholders. For some, this represents an effort to achieve a missing balance. (A government stakeholder observed, *"There is a perception that NEJAC is very EJ-friendly."* Indeed, several industry stakeholders suggested more business and local government consultation. By contrast, a community representative strongly argued that more industry and State representation in NEJAC would unbalance the Council, making it resemble other Federal advisory committees which offer communities token representation diluted by the sheer number of other participants.) For others, though, going beyond NEJAC is simply a way to win broad acceptance of any NEJAC recommendations. Several stakeholders stated that it is important to look more broadly even within EPA itself; e.g., *"All departments and programs within the Agency should be discussing [this issue]."*

Finally, one stakeholder commented that the choice of forum was unimportant. *"It can be any forum as long as EPA listens."*

3. The overall goal of environmental permitting.

Stakeholders differed in their view of the appropriate overall Agency goal in permitting. When asked whether the permit agency should address pre-existing conditions with potential health or environmental impacts in permitting, community stakeholders reply simply and emphatically *"Yes!"* They cited communities where *"shelter in place"* alarms are a regular feature of community life. *("Shelter in place"* refers to governmental strategies which seek to minimize human exposure to high air pollutant episodes by recommending residents go inside whenever an alarm whistle is sounded.) To community stakeholders, this signified that *"the system is broken.... There is no study which proves that "shelter in place" works, that [ordinary residential] structures adequately protect people...."* They stressed the need for meaningful planning and siting so that the number of people adversely affected in a worst-case pollution scenario is minimized or eliminated.

The Tribal, State, local government, and academic stakeholders agreed that permit agencies should address pre-existing conditions. One emphasized these factors *"may be more important than sporadic permit issues."* Another added that such considerations *"should not be an afterthought, but should be raised early in the process and used as a guideline for determining whether any [siting] action should be taken at all."* A third concluded, *"A responsible agency looking out for the community's interests should relatively level the playing field."*

Collectively, these stakeholders offered a variety of recommendations for addressing pre-existing conditions. They suggested that, where facilities are sited in or near residential areas, permitting agencies:

(1) Assess community vulnerability. Typical comments included: *"We need to have a good sense of the existing baseline;" "There ought to be an inventory of pre-existing adverse conditions which shows that [some communities] experience a substantially inferior environment;" "Where you have a vulnerable population (for example, where the incidence of asthma is high), a responsible agency official should be circumspect about permitting another air emitter."*

(2) Identify and weigh cumulative risks, including those associated with a worst-case spill or incident. (Admittedly, quantifying the degree of risk would require better research on both the effects of pollutants and synergism among pollutants.)

(3) Consider future as well as existing projects. One stakeholder called for *"a future allocation mechanism"* to ensure that the first applicant doesn't absorb all of a neighborhood's potential for growth (e.g., traffic capacity).

(4) Require applicants for new or modified permits to ask: What modifications are necessary to address environmental justice impacts or cumulative risks?

(5) Gather and assess economic and demographic data in permitting to ensure that adverse uses don't get disproportionately located among minorities and poor people.

(6) Establish a budget for addressing pre-existing conditions. One stakeholder warned: *"Any attempt to deal with pre-existing conditions has to be accompanied by a budget."*

Industry stakeholders approached this environmental justice goal more cautiously. They acknowledged *"agencies have to deal with cumulative risk in some fashion,"* but stressed the need for *"legal authority," "clear criteria for injustice," "enough information on emissions and health effects to make clear calls," "[and avoiding having] the system bog down."* They questioned whether *"agencies have the resources to have permit writers become fully conversant with these issues"* and emphasized that different perceptions on the issues may exist even within the local community, further complicating review.

Nonetheless, industrial stakeholders shared with other stakeholders a willingness to explore approaches to environmental justice in permitting. While not endorsing any particular solution, industry stakeholders raised the following possibilities:

(1) Permit agencies can examine, document, and help raise awareness of pre-existing conditions.

(2) There could be further public scrutiny of zoning and land use planning for environmental justice impacts.

(3) Agencies could publicize more information on what factors contribute to successful brownfields projects.

(4) Rather than subject all permits -- even minor permits -- to full-blown cumulative impact analysis, agencies could screen permits to determine which merit fuller scrutiny because of the size of the source, toxicity of the emissions, or degree of public interest in the outcome.

(5) Corporate policies on siting and acquisition could be changed so that environmental personnel are integrated into decision-making earlier in the process, before companies are so heavily invested in a particular site. (Under current practice, siting is primarily market-driven. Only after a lengthy analysis of non-environmental factors, such as access to supplies and transportation corridors, growth

potential, etc., does a company look at the community, its environment and quality of life.)

(6) Where high risks exist due to prior land use planning errors, successful relocation efforts and voluntary buy-outs could be examined. In the Netherlands, for example, when cumulative risk analysis indicated that community exposure crossed a specified threshold, the government devised a 5-10 year community relocation plan. Voluntary buy-outs to expand buffer zones around industrial facilities have also occurred in the United States.

In general, EPA stakeholders agreed with the goal of addressing cumulative environmental impacts in permitting (assuming legal authority to do so). Some, however, expressed interest in limiting such analysis to major permits, "cancer alleys," or "hot spots," while others appeared to embrace it for a broader universe of permits. Several recommended greater attention to the environmental impacts of zoning and planning decisions, and other stakeholders concurred.

4. The focus of current permitting.

The stakeholders shared differing views as to what now transpires in the permit process. Industry stakeholders saw the current process as largely centered on technical issues of compliance with federal and state discharge regulations. Government stakeholders saw themselves addressing a somewhat broader set of issues -- still largely centered on compliance with technology requirements, but also encompassing public participation, protection of health and the environment, interagency coordination, enforcement, and state oversight. In marked contrast, Tribal and community stakeholders saw the process as exceedingly narrow, ignoring treaty rights and community views -- indeed, driven toward a distinctly (from their view) biased result. One cited situations where facility construction is underway while the permit application is purportedly still being considered: *"Companies wouldn't invest this money if they didn't feel they could get their permit."* Another put it: *"The process proceeds with an eye toward nothing but technical compliance with numbers and, if there is not compliance, then how can we help the facility get its permit?"* At least one EPA stakeholder appeared to agree: *"If the objective [of the community] is to stop the permit altogether, ... it is hard for EPA to share that goal. Our goal is to make sure these sources have permits, unless they don't comply [with applicable regulations]."*

All stakeholders, however, agreed that, absent a stronger or more comprehensive state statute, the current process does not address the type of environmental justice concerns being raised by Tribal and community organizations. One EPA official summarized, *"There is not a wit given to environmental justice issues [in permitting]."*

Even where states look at cumulative impacts (for example, under a state NEPA-type statute), the analysis tends to be cursory in comparison to the issues raised by environmental justice groups. As one stakeholder put it, *"We are better at looking at project-specific impacts than we are at looking at the cumulative impacts of related projects. Even when we try to do so, we fall short.... We tend to jump directly to mitigation. With environmental justice especially, we need to go back to how to avoid impacts, then how to minimize them, and then mitigation. There is a hierarchy there.... We also need to ask what are the real objectives of the project? What alternatives are we required to consider under the law? We seldom look at how these are written. But if they are not broad, then we don't look at issues of alternatives."*

5. The limitations of the current permit program,

The most frequently cited problems with the current permit program were: (1) the failure to consider environmental justice or cumulative impacts; (2) the absence of clear authority (either from explicit statutory language or official Agency legal interpretation) to address environmental justice in permitting; and (3) the lack of adequate public participation.

Other problems stakeholders mentioned included fundamental weaknesses in the level of protection provided by the underlying regulatory standards and failure to obtain pre-decisional input from Native American Tribes. One stakeholder also questioned whether existing sources, less subject to intense scrutiny in permit proceedings, weren't often more of a problem than the more thoroughly reviewed new sources.

6. Stakeholder involvement in the permit program.

While all stakeholders agreed on the importance of community involvement in permitting, EPA stakeholders tended to differ from others over the adequacy of current public participation.

Non-Agency stakeholders agreed that the current program does not adequately include community input. Industry stakeholders ranked the process *"not a good job"* to *"terrible."* They criticized: (1) the inadequate publicity *("It's not in the local papers, what the community reads.")*; (2) failure to address language barriers; (3) lack of efficiency in public meetings *("They're time wasters; they lack focus.")*; (4) heavy and unnecessary reliance on technical language; (5) poor outreach *("The same old [stakeholder representatives] are always consulted")*; and (6) poor timing: *"The timing is all wrong. Thirty days at the end of the process makes no sense when the company and agency have been negotiating together for years. The agencies should move it up. "* One noted that Agency staff suffer from the same syndrome as corporate personnel: *"It is a tough thing for plant managers to swallow when the little lady next door has the right answer."* This stakeholder also observed, *"Technical people are often unqualified to run public meetings. They often try to devise technical solutions to what are essentially relationship problems."*

When asked whether agencies now do a good job, a community stakeholder responded *"resoundingly no!"* This community representative faulted agencies for *"absolute reluctance and resistance ... to meet,"* and for not *"listening and incorporating stakeholder concerns. For example, they say 'we have an approach to deal with this problem without any input.... Take it or leave it'."* Another, noting that *"EPA has come a long way, "* stated, *"I want to be respectful of what has been done, but things could be moving a lot faster."* This stakeholder observed a tendency in some Regions to do *"just enough to get by."*

Tribes, too, felt uninvolved at meaningful stages of the process. Academic, State and local government stakeholders also identified public participation as an area in need of strengthening.

EPA stakeholders presented a different picture. While some confessed the Agency does a poor job of stimulating public involvement, most rank the Agency's performance as *"okay," "getting better, "* or varied depending upon the State or location. Several cited the *"many opportunities"* for public involvement, the *"clear open door, "* and the *"stakeholder-driven"* nature of the Agency. Several stakeholders, however, noted with concern a growing tension between demands upon EPA from Congress and other stakeholders to streamline the permit process, on the one hand, and conflicting pressure to slow down to include more public participation.

Regardless of how they viewed the current process, stakeholders identified similar criteria for determining whether the public participation process is working:

- Public knowledge of pending permit decisions would be more widespread. *("It would be a long time since you heard the complaint that I didn't know [about this proceeding] and they wouldn't listen to me.")*
- *"The community would be showing up at meetings."*
- The public would be *"informed enough to participate effectively."*
- Proceedings would be characterized by *"meaningful dialogue"* on community issues. Communities would suggest operating conditions and other adjustments in facility operations.
- *"Permits [would] more regularly respond to individual community needs."*
- *"Ongoing, continuing communications"* would occur between stakeholders, perhaps even after permit issuance.
- There would be greater indicators of community satisfaction with the process (E.g., *"People would feel heard and heard early in the process."* One stakeholder suggested EPA survey for such indicators, *"You could ask stakeholders after-the-fact, 'Did you have the information you needed'?"* EPA could then examine responses to outline a successful model.)
- There would be greater satisfaction among EPA's own Regional Environmental Justice Coordinators.
- Permit writers also would feel satisfied. They would *"be able to look at all affected populations and feel comfortable that they understood and had input."*
- *"See what happens to the pollution loading. Is it coming down? Is there real world progress or just messing around with public participation?"*

A community stakeholder had specific recommendations for achieving better participation: a commitment to public participation at the Regional Administrator level in all regions, in-depth training of Agency personnel at all levels, and additional resources for communities to do their own training and to acquire technical assistance (legal, scientific, medical, etc.). This stakeholder commented, *"You can't talk about equality when you have one side with resources and the other with none. The Agency has to be prepared to assist in balancing the equality."*

7. Facilitating stakeholder cooperation.

While stakeholders acknowledged that the current permit process can be adversarial -- at times needlessly so, they generally rejected casting the solution as a search for a more cooperative permitting model. A community stakeholder stated flatly, *"It's not a matter of finding a more cooperative mechanism... The struggle comes in because the community feels that it is not being treated properly."* A government stakeholder explained: *"The amount of conflict should not be a criterion. Conflict could be a sign of a healthy process."* An industry representative amplified: *"The issue is not cooperation. People need a platform to be heard. They need to have their questions and concerns addressed. If that happens, people can accept a technical answer better. They will still disagree, but not violently."* As one industry stakeholder explained, the issue of cooperation is really one of finding better ways to facilitate communication: *"We need better communication. That will lead to cooperation."*

In general, most EPA stakeholders tended to view facilitated Alternative Dispute Resolution (ADR) as potentially helpful in certain high controversy permit proceedings -- if done effectively, and therefore worthy of further exploration. However, other stakeholders warned against too eager or sweeping an embrace of ADR.

For example, industry stakeholders viewed the utility of ADR as dependent, to a great extent, on the problem-solving, communication, and persuasion skills of the facilitator: *"It could help. It depends on who's doing it. Ideally, you want the lines of communication to include some sense of what the community wants."* Another echoed: *"Some people are terrible at it. Problem-solving requires certain skills; you have to have them."* An academic stakeholder agreed: *"This is an area that is ripe for ADR ... [but also] a challenging area for ADR. If the ADR people tend to look and act condescending to the environmental justice representatives, trust evaporates immediately."*

Academic stakeholders warned that ADR can *"be troubling as a response [in view of] power disparities [between the facility and the community];"* they suggested *"ADR has no real integrity until you equalize the playing field,"* but admitted it is difficult to craft appropriate *"safeguards."* A Tribal representative also cautioned that, while ADR *"used properly is an effective tool,"* used improperly it can be *"a tool to coerce based on a 'panel of experts' opinions'."*

A community stakeholder described ADR as *"nothing more than process ... trying to get to yes when they never considered why the community would say no.... The issue is not properly framed.... It's not a matter of finding a more cooperative mechanism.... Antagonism exists now because the agency and the facility are unwilling to consider significant changes and the 'no project' option."* Another cautioned, *"ADR may hinder.... It depends on the situation and the process the parties went through - whether they will trust [ADR]."*

Indeed, lack of trust appeared as a serious obstacle to further use of ADR. An industry representative summarized: *"Corporations are nervous about giving away too much. Attorneys don't like unless they're doing it. Communities either fear giving away too much or else they're not comfortable. If the ADR person is paid by the company or the government, communities assume he or she will hold their [paying] views in higher regard."*

But trust is not the only obstacle. ADR also requires resources and time. An industry spokesman explained: *"Going public takes more time which is often inconsistent with business needs. To speed up [public involvement], you have to start early and have an infrastructure to support it."* A government stakeholder also warned: *"ADR is a lengthy process and it doesn't necessarily resolve the dispute."*

Several stakeholders cautioned that success with ADR requires more definition of the underlying ground rules of the transaction. One explained: *"ADR begs the question. It's like asking an arbitrator to resolve a claim without providing the information that may lead to an agreement. It may be a good safety valve, ... [but] the real concern is that the rules of the road are unclear."* Another agreed: *"The parties start from different premises without settled law. Everyone is afraid to negotiate anything away, especially at the beginning."* A third echoed the need for EPA leadership: *"EPA needs to decide the parameters of the box.... EPA can set people up to fail if they don't set forth ... the ground rules and time constraints. If they just say, 'Let's all get together and solve the problem' without any consequences, people come together but there is no reason to come to agreement."* One stakeholder concluded that agencies need to know what they are doing when they embrace ADR or other facilitation techniques so as not to frustrate environmental justice communities anew: *"When you promise a new solution, you can breed further unhappiness if you don't solve the problem."*

8. Expanding the horizons of current permitting.

Three (3) recommendations for improving the current permit process emerged continually in these interviews. The first relates to expanded public involvement. As one stakeholder put it, *"People feel not welcomed or taken seriously. Everyone agrees we ought to fix that."* The second relates to consideration of cumulative impacts. The third involves clarifying the permit writer's obligations. All three (3) are discussed below.

a. Expanded public involvement.

Stakeholders frequently recommended improvements in: (1) timing of public involvement; (2) agency and company responsiveness to communities; and (3) conduct of public meetings.

Typical comments from industry stakeholders on the timing of public comment included the following:

- *"Often the largest challenge is creating a credible public dialogue. The earlier this occurs, the better the public is served. The later it happens, the more the public feels left out, that the deal is done."*
- *"The current system requires public input, but only late in the process. This tends to create an adversarial environment rather than an open public dialogue because of the lateness. It leaves the public feeling that its vote didn't count, that they weren't heard -- and it's true to some extent."*
- *"There is ample room for creative expansion of notice (TV, bulletin boards, etc.) This is not rocket science. It's deciding it's worth it."*

Community stakeholders agreed. One stated: *"Permittees talk to the agency on a daily basis for years before the first public hearing. It's only human nature; [the agency staff] don't want to hear what's wrong with a permit they have spent two years writing. They should have a hearing on the day of the application and give everyone whatever information they have."*

Industry stakeholders also recommended that companies listen more effectively to communities. One stated: *"Companies should make a commitment to respond in writing with a report to each question and a copy to anyone who wants one. They can supply an interim report if they don't have answers to all the questions right then."* This echoed community sentiments that agencies and companies give mere *"lip service"* to their comments.

Finally, industry and community stakeholders recommended that EPA improve the quality of public meetings. An industry representative stated, *"EPA is terrible at running public meetings. Their very nature tends to create an adversary environment. There is technology in mediating and facilitating a public forum, but the agency hasn't embraced it. "* A community representative agreed: *"Usually, it's one A.M. before[permit] opponents have a chance to testify."*

      b. Identification of cumulative impacts.

All stakeholders agreed that environmental agencies -- whether through permitting, regulation, or cooperation with land use agencies -- need to address cumulative impacts in some fashion. Permit writers, in particular, decry the lack of tools and guidance on how to accomplish this task.

      c. Clarifying the permit writer's obligations.

Stakeholders agreed that there is also a need to define more clearly what the permit writer should do when confronted with disparate treatment. Government stakeholders frequently cited their lack of authority to reject projects on environmental justice grounds. Community stakeholders, by contrast, claimed that Agency staff have not been asked to respond creatively to Office of General Counsel guidance identifying existing statutory authority. An industry stakeholder summarized, *"On the substance, there is real intellectual bankruptcy. What are the rules of the road? What does the Executive Order forbid? What is the basis of a Title VI complaint? What is the right thing to do? Companies fear that projects will be abandoned or delayed without reason and that others will go forward where they shouldn't..... There is no coherent understanding of what we're trying to do."* Taken together, these comments suggest the need for additional legal guidance -- presumably from the Office of General Counsel -- in this area.

9. Opportunities for mutual stakeholder gain.

Industry stakeholders were optimistic about the possibility of identifying opportunities for mutual stakeholder gain. One stated: *"There are lots of win-win opportunities. You can get people talking, get companies to be better corporate neighbors, enhance community involvement."* Examples of opportunities these stakeholders envision included: *"certainty that a company can get a permit and operate within it,"* avoiding *"after-the-fact Title VI complaints which drive companies crazy [by] upfront discussions to surface and resolve problems,"* *"making companies pay more attention to communities,"* and identifying *"opportunities for emission offsets [that reflect] the community's understanding of the emission sources [most strongly] impacting their lives."* Industry also saw unexplored benefits for communities: *"The continued operation of a well-run facility brings employment and secondary benefits from jobs. Facilities attract support services and other facilities."* In addition, *"facilities can do things for communities that the city may not do ... such as addressing suppliers' driving habits."*

Industry stakeholders cautioned, however, that consensus is possible only up to a point. As one stated: *"You can't control what people want. It goes back to expectations. Neighborhood control over who can operate there is not realistic, but better outreach, process, safety, housekeeping is all doable."* Another clarified that impasse-type situations comprise only a small percentage of permit applications : *"The [current] process is not broken, though it might not be adequate. But it is broken on the highly controversial issues. Where a company does a sneak attack with the application, that's when people get frustrated. Ninety-nine of one hundred permits happen without contest. A whole lot of permits involve only minor modifications of a facility. The controversy centers around siting ... or where a facility has already ticked off the community. But these are the exceptions rather than the rule."*

Community stakeholders also sensed some opportunities for mutual gain. One stated: *"We want industries that want to be good neighbors.... From a proactive side, it is worth it to spend time on what we want it to be like - envisioning our communities."* Another added: *"The process could be revamped to take multiple, cumulative, synergistic impacts into account. We could also create buffer zones. The agency has the authority to be more protective than it is now.... We could change ways of thinking in industry and the agencies. Industry could see profits go up with cleaner facilities. Agencies could say 'do we have discretionary authority to address this problem,' [rather than] 'show me a direct mandate'."*

21

These stakeholders' optimism, too, was edged with realism. *"It's not that toxic facilities will go elsewhere, but we can find a way to produce products without sacrifice to health and the environment. The ultimate goal is sustainable development, not dead-end, extractable, exploitative development."* A Tribal stakeholder cautioned, *"When you balance the economy versus the ecology, this has to be done in small steps, carefully thought through, with the involvement of the entire community. You need input early, upfront, and as a guideline for the eventual decision."*

10. Community monitoring of compliance.

Stakeholders differed markedly in their initial responses to questions about community monitoring of facility compliance, though the differences may have had more to do with whether their response was focused on ensuring technical compliance or enhancing program credibility.

Community, Tribal, state, local government, and academic stakeholders, for the most part, enthusiastically endorsed community monitoring of facility compliance. They cited a variety of obvious, as well as innovative, ways to accomplish this objective, including:
   a. bucket brigades in which citizens learn how to collect and send samples to EPA-approved labs (used as the basis for at least one successful enforcement action in Region IX),
   b. requiring companies with continuous emission monitoring to have digital printouts on stacks reporting their emission limits,
   c. Community Advisory Committees,
   d. monitoring and enforcement by other governmental entities (e.g., Tribes and local governments),
   e. use of qualified consultants,
   f. community-facility good neighbor agreements, and
   g. daily posting of compliance data on the web.

A community representative pointed out that *"the Agency can't be everywhere"* and that citizen monitoring *"from the front porch"* can be maintained over longer time intervals than temporary Agency monitors. This stakeholder also observed that many community groups distrusted Agency enforcement personnel as *"dismissive"* of their concerns and suspected that *"it's a rare instance where monitoring doesn't show a violation."*

Industry stakeholders were willing to entertain proposals for community monitoring, but expressed caution about issues such as inadequate data quality, errors in data transmission, collection of data which is unwanted and unused, and the risk of citizen suits. Nonetheless, industry stakeholders accepted the fact that compliance data will be made public.

Industry stakeholders also recognized that the issue of community monitoring of compliance is intertwined with the notion of trust. As one stakeholder put it, *"Communities don't want to run the company. They want to be listened to and have their questions answered. If you establish a trust relationship, the community will rely on you to do the job. If you don't, you can't possibly supply enough data."* This may explain why industry stakeholders were not adverse to exploring ways to enhance community trust in compliance data -- for example, sending a community representative into a facility to read monitoring dials or requiring companies to respond to community questions about compliance.

EPA stakeholders as a group expressed the greatest skepticism to community compliance monitoring. One stated *"Community policing is best left to the regulatory agency."* Others *"doubt[ed] its effectiveness,"* questioned the expense and practicality, cited the difficulties in training citizens, saw themselves as already addressing the need (by requiring companies to submit annual reports to the community), or saw additional requirements as unnecessary because citizens are already using monitoring data to file enforcement suits or urge EPA to step up enforcement.

It is not clear, however, that EPA stakeholders would differ so substantially from other stakeholders if the goal were enhanced facility-governmental-community relations as opposed to mere technical compliance with regulatory standards. Most EPA stakeholders were not familiar with situations in which community monitoring had either assisted the agency or increased public acceptance of the regulatory program. If community monitoring proposals were tailored to accomplish these ends, they might have garnered more support from EPA. As one EPA official put it, *"if it would reduce suspicion,"* then community monitoring would be helpful.

11. Additional issues.

Most stakeholders expressed satisfaction with the scope of the interview questions. Several suggested additional areas of inquiry, including but not limited to the following:

a. How to promote agency awareness of, and response to, the Office of General Counsel's identification of EJ opportunities under existing statutes and how to get permit writers to begin utilizing these opportunities.

b. How to address environmental justice in *"all of the program decisions that stack the deck by the time you get to permitting ... (i.e., program design, policy formation)."*

c. How to start looking at not just the permit process, but the *"implementation level of permitting ... what's happening day to day... go further into the nuts and bolts. This could raise a plethora of issues."*

d. How to address cross-agency coordination, engaging other federal agencies (e.g., HUD), state agencies and local health departments in addressing environmental justice (including funding states).

e. How to develop a national policy to ensure State consistency in addressing disparate impacts, in order to avoid industrial forum shopping for lax regulatory jurisdictions.

f. How to distinguish between competing objectives, defining not only a vision of success, but also priorities and intermediate steps for achieving the vision.

g. How to determine which sources pose the biggest risks for environmental justice communities (i.e. permits for new sources or small, existing, mobile, or other sources) in order to target agency resources and maximize risk reduction.

h. How better to incorporate input from Tribes, which occupy a unique status as sovereign stakeholders and which differ from each other in terms of religion, culture, and ways of living.

i. How to address the need for jobs -- and good ones -- in environmental justice communities. E.g., *"The number one factor in life expectancy/longevity is poverty. Poverty doesn't get factored in well."*

CONCLUSION

The stakeholders surveyed here shared many common concerns -- and fundamental disagreements -- over where and how to address environmental justice concerns regarding permitting. Nonetheless, the degree of accord suggests that there are promising opportunities for consensus on recommendations which enhance the capacity of the current permit process to respond to stakeholders' needs regarding environmental justice.

Accord was greatest on issues related to better public outreach, expanded community participation in decision-making, greater assurances of industry compliance, and greater attention to cumulative risks. Stakeholders differed more sharply over a community's right to prevent siting of a facility which otherwise complies with applicable regulatory standards. However, stakeholders acknowledged that these situations represent a small percentage of permit applications and can frequently be avoided by changed industry and government behavior (such as early involvement of environmental personnel in internal corporate decision-making and community representatives in government decision-making.) For the bulk of permit decisions, the stakeholders surveyed here have laid the foundation for an ample set of recommendations for EPA review.

Attachment 1
List of Interviewed Stakeholders

EPA:

Tim Fields
Assistant Administrator
Office of Solid Waste and Emergency Response
(OSWER)

Rob Brenner
Acting Deputy Assistant Administrator
Office of Air and Radiation (OAR)

Vernon Myers
Environmental Scientist
Office of Solid Waste and Emergency Response
(OSWER)

Freya Margand
Environmental Protection Specialist
Office of Solid Waste and Emergency Response
(OSWER)

Anna Wood
Regulatory Impact Analyst
Office of Air and Radiation (OAR)

Bob Kellam
Associate Director
Information Transfer and Program Integration
Division
Office of Air and Radiation (OAR)

Rosanna Hoffman
Attorney Advisor
Office of Water

Tom Voltaggio
Region III Deputy Regional Administrator

Tribal/State/Local Government:

Stuart Harris
Cultural Resources Coordinator
for the Special Science and Resources Program
Confederated Tribes of the Umatilla Indian
Reservation

Robert Varney
Commissioner
New Hampshire Department of Environment

Andrea Kreiner
Manager, Business and Permitting Services Office

Delaware Department of Natural Resources &
Environmental Control

Lillian Kawasaki
General Manager
City of Los Angeles Department of Environmental
Affairs

Russell Harding (could not be interviewed due to
scheduling conflicts)
Director
Michigan Department of Environmental Quality

Industry:

Pat Hill
Senior Manager
Georgia Pacific

Michael Steinberg
Attorney at Law (Partner)
Morgan, Lewis & Bockius

Jerry Martin
Vice President & Global Director of EJ&S
Regulatory Affairs
Dow Chemical Company

Community:

Richard Moore
Director
Southwest Network for Environmental and
Economic Justice

Nathalie Walker
Managing Attorney
Earthjustice Legal Defense Fund

Deeohn Ferris (could not be interviewed due to
scheduling conflicts)
Owner
Global Environmental Resources, Inc.

Academic:

Richard Lazarus
Professor
Georgetown University Law Center

Yale Rabin
Professor

Massachusetts Institute of Technology

Eileen Gauna
Professor
Southwestern Law School

Attachment 2
Interview Questions

1. How important is the issue of incorporating environmental justice considerations in environmental permitting?
2. Is NEJAC the appropriate forum for initiating a dialogue on this policy question?
3. What are the most important factors, or categories of factors, that the permitting authority now considers when making a permitting decision?
4. What are the problems (both substantive and procedural) with the permitting process in terms of addressing environmental justice issues?
5. What types of factors, if any, should the permitting authority consider to help ensure environmental justice in permitting?
6. Should the permit authority address pre-existing potential health or environmental conditions in the affected community with respect to permit actions? If so, how (e.g., through cumulative impacts analysis, siting criteria, assessment of vulnerable or sensitive populations, or some other mechanism)?
7. (a) Is stakeholder involvement in the permitting process important to the development of good decision-making or important for other reasons (other than to satisfy legal requirements)?

   (b) Is the permitting process now doing a good job of involving the public at large, and environmental justice populations in particular, in permit decision-making?

   (c) What are the three things that EPA and/or the permitting authority does best to involve stakeholders in the permitting process and the three things they do least well?

   (d) Are there improvements you could suggest?

   (e) How would you assess whether the process is working well at involving stakeholders in a meaningful manner?
8. (a) Does the current permitting process encourage cooperative or adversarial relationships among stakeholders? Would a process that encourages cooperation be advantageous?

   (b) Would dispute resolution techniques help or hinder the permitting process?

   (c) What are the obstacles to use of dispute resolution?
9. (a) What are your most important needs from the permitting process?

   (b) Are there opportunities in the permit process for mutual community/industry gain?

   (c) What could be done to encourage such opportunities?
10. (a) Would permit terms and conditions providing for community monitoring of compliance   be of use?

(b) Are there instances where community monitoring has improved compliance or the relationship between the permitted facility and other stakeholders?

11. How should the Agency address quality of life issues and risk communication in the permit process?

12. Are there other questions NEJAC should be asking about this topic? Other suggestions you would like to make?

###

United States
Environmental Protection
Agency

Enforcement and
Compliance Assurance
(2201A)

EPA 300-S-00-003
March 2000
www.epa.gov

Office of Environmental Justice (OEJ)

♻EPA Summary of the Meeting of the National Environmental Justice Advisory Council

A FEDERAL ADVISORY COMMITTEE

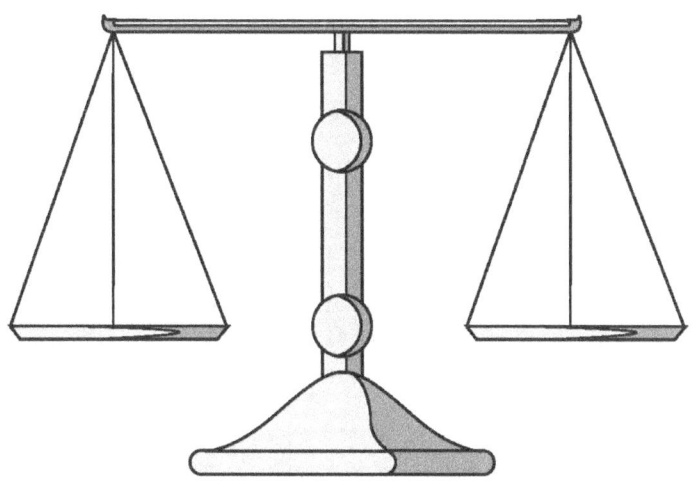

EXECUTIVE SUMMARY

Hilton Crystal City at National Airport
Arlington, Virginia
November 30 through December 2, 1999

PREFACE

The National Environmental Justice Advisory Council (NEJAC) is a federal advisory committee that was established by charter on September 30, 1993, to provide independent advice, consultation, and recommendations to the Administrator of the U.S. Environmental Protection Agency (EPA) on matters related to environmental justice. The NEJAC is made up of 25 members, and one DFO, who serve on a parent council that has six subcommittees. Along with the NEJAC members who fill subcommittee posts, an additional 39 individuals serve on the various subcommittees. To date, NEJAC has held fourteen meetings in the following locations:

- Washington, D.C., May 20, 1994

- Albuquerque, New Mexico, August 3 through 5, 1994

- Herndon, Virginia, October 25 through 27, 1994

- Atlanta, Georgia, January 17 and 18, 1995

- Arlington, Virginia, July 25 and 26, 1995

- Washington, D.C., December 12 through 14, 1995

- Detroit, Michigan, May 29 through 31, 1996

- Baltimore, Maryland, December 10 through 12, 1996

- Wabeno, Wisconsin, May 13 through 15, 1997

- Durham, North Carolina, December 8 through 10, 1997

- Arlington, Virginia, February 23 through 24, 1998 (Special Business Meeting)

- Oakland, California, May 31 through June 2, 1998

- Baton Rouge, Louisiana, December 7 through 10, 1998

- Arlington, Virginia, November 30 through December 2, 1999

The NEJAC also has held other meetings which include:

- Public Dialogues on Urban Revitalization and Brownfields: Envisioning Healthy and Sustainable Communities held in Boston, Massachusetts; Philadelphia, Pennsylvania; Detroit, Michigan; Oakland, California; and Atlanta, Georgia in the Summer 1995

- Relocation Roundtable, Pensacola, Florida, May 2 through 4, 1996

- Environmental Justice Enforcement and Compliance Assurance Roundtable, San Antonio, Texas, October 17 through 19, 1996

- Environmental Justice Enforcement Roundtable, Durham, North Carolina, December 11 through 13, 1997

- International Roundtable on Environmental Justice on the U.S./Mexico Border, San Diego, California, August 19 through 21, 1999.

As a federal advisory committee, the NEJAC is bound by all requirements of the Federal Advisory Committee Act (FACA) of October 6, 1972. Those requirements include:

- Members must be selected and appointed by EPA

- Members must attend and participate fully in meetings of NEJAC

- Meetings must be open to the public, except as specified by the Administrator

- All meetings must be announced in the Federal Register

- Public participation must be allowed at all public meetings

i

- The public must be provided access to materials distributed during the meeting

- Meeting minutes must be kept and made available to the public

- A designated federal official (DFO) must be present at all meetings of the NEJAC (and its subcommittees)

- NEJAC must provide independent judgment that is not influenced by special interest groups

Each subcommittee, formed to deal with a specific topic and to facilitate the conduct of the business of NEJAC, has a DFO and is bound by the requirements of FACA. Subcommittees of the NEJAC meet independently of the full NEJAC and present their findings to the NEJAC for review. Subcommittees cannot make recommendations independently to EPA. In addition to the six subcommittees, the NEJAC has established a Protocol Committee, the members of which are the chair of NEJAC and the chairs of each subcommittee.

Members of the NEJAC are presented in the table on the following page. A list of the members of each of the six subcommittees are presented in the appropriate chapters of the report.

NATIONAL ENVIRONMENTAL JUSTICE ADVISORY COUNCIL
MEMBERS OF THE EXECUTIVE COUNCIL
(1999)

Designated Federal Official:
Mr. Charles Lee, Associate Director for Policy and Interagency Liason, EPA Office of Environmental Justice

Chair:
Mr. Haywood Turrentine

Members

Mr. Don Aragon	Ms. Annabelle Jaramillo
Ms. Rose Marie Augustine	Ms. Vernice Miller-Travis
Ms. Leslie Ann Beckoff Cormier	Mr. David Moore
Ms. Sue Briggum	Dr. Marinelle Payton
Mr. Dwayne Beavers	Mr. Gerald Prout
Mr. Luke Cole	Ms. Rosa Hilda Ramos
Mr. Fernando Cuevas, Sr.	Ms. Peggy Shepard
Ms. Rosa Franklin	Ms. Jane Stahl
Mr. Arnoldo Garcia	Mr. Gerald Torres
Dr. Michel Gelobter	Mr. Damon Whitehead
Mr. Tom Goldtooth	Ms. Margaret Williams
Ms. Jennifer Hill-Kelley	Mr. Tseming Yang

EPA's Office of Environmental Justice (OEJ) maintains transcripts, summary reports, and other material distributed during the meetings. Those documents are available to the public upon request.

Comments or questions can be directed to OEJ through the Internet. OEJ's Internet E-mail address is:

environmental-justice-epa@.epa.gov

Executive Summaries of the reports of the NEJAC meetings are available in English and Spanish on the Internet at the NEJAC's World Wide Web home page:

http://www.epa.gov/oeca/main/ej/nejac/index.html> (click on the publications icon)

EXECUTIVE SUMMARY

INTRODUCTION

This executive summary provides highlights of the fourteenth meeting of the National Environmental Justice Advisory Council (NEJAC), held November 30 through December 2, 1999 at the Hilton Crystal City at National Airport in Arlington, Virginia. Each of the six subcommittees met for a full day on December 1, 1999. The NEJAC hosted on November 30 a public comment period which focused on issues related to environmental justice and the issuance of environmental permits. The NEJAC also hosted on December 1 a second public comment period for general environmental justice issues. Approximately 400 persons attended the meetings and the public comment periods.

The NEJAC is a federal advisory committee that was established by charter on September 30, 1993 to provide independent advice, consultation, and recommendations to the Administrator of the U.S. Environmental Protection Agency (EPA) on matters related to environmental justice. Mr. Haywood Turrentine, Laborers' District Council Education and Training Trust Fund (an affiliate of the Laborers' International Union of North America), serves as the chair of the Executive Council. Mr. Charles Lee, Associate Director for Policy and Interagency Liaison, EPA Office of Environmental Justice (OEJ), serves as the Designated Federal Official (DFO) for the Executive Council. Exhibit ES-1 lists the chair and DFO of the executive council, as well as the persons who chair the six subcommittees of the NEJAC and the EPA staff appointed to serve as the DFOs for the subcommittees.

OEJ maintains transcripts and summary reports of the proceedings of the NEJAC meetings. Those documents are available to the public upon request. The public also has access to the executive summaries of reports of previous meetings, as well as other publications of the NEJAC, through the World Wide Web at <http://www.epa.gov/oeca/main/ej/nejac/index.html> (click on the publications icon). The summaries are available in both English- and Spanish-language versions.

<table>
<tr><td align="right">Exhibit ES-1</td></tr>
<tr><td>

NATIONAL ENVIRONMENTAL JUSTICE ADVISORY COUNCIL CHAIRS AND DESIGNATED FEDERAL OFFICIALS (DFO)

Executive Council:
    Mr. Haywood Turrentine, **Chair**
    Mr. Charles Lee, **DFO**

Air and Water Subcommittee:
    Dr. Michel Gelobter, **Chair**
    Ms. Alice Walker, **co-DFO**
    Dr. Wil Wilson, **co-DFO**

Enforcement Subcommittee:
    Mr. Luke Cole, **Chair**
    Ms. Shirley Pate, **DFO**

Health and Research Subcommittee:
    Dr. Marinelle Payton, **Chair**
    Mr. Lawrence Martin, **co-DFO**
    Mr. Chen Wen, **co-DFO**

Indigenous Peoples Subcommittee:
    Mr. Tom Goldtooth, **Chair**
    Mr. Daniel Gogal, **Acting DFO**
    Mr. Anthony Hanson, **Alternate DFO**

International Subcommittee:
    Mr. Arnoldo Garcia, **Chair**
    Ms. Wendy Graham, **DFO**

Waste and Facility Siting Subcommittee:
    Ms. Vernice Miller-Travis, **Chair**
    Mr. Kent Benjamin, **DFO**

</td></tr>
</table>

REMARKS

Ms. Carol Browner, Administrator, EPA, extended her appreciation to representatives of EPA and members of the NEJAC who have been working on addressing issues related to environmental justice at the agency. She stated that addressing environmental justice is not an easy task and one that is not becoming easier to address as new evidence is identified that minority and low-income communities do bear a disproportionate "brunt of [the impacts of] our modern technological society." She emphasized the need for the members of the NEJAC to stay focused on the topic of this meeting. Ms. Browner expressed her belief that when decision-makers truly engage a local community, up front and in an informed and meaningful manner, the quality of the decision that the agency or other regulatory entity is able to make is dramatically improved compared to a decision that is made without the engagement of the community. She continued by saying that the challenge that lays before EPA is how to involve a local community in an effective, open, honest, and informed manner.

Ms. Browner concluded her remarks by stating that the agency needs to take a "real look" at the regulatory decisions made as well as the guidance and framework that EPA issues to state and local governments to ensure that principles related to environmental justice are being integrated into the decision-making process for issuing permits.

Mr. Steven Herman, Assistant Administrator, EPA Office of Enforcement and Compliance Assurance (OECA), expressed the agency's continuous appreciation to the members of the NEJAC for their invaluable assistance in providing EPA advice and counsel on issues related to environmental justice. Mr. Herman then noted the change in format for this and future meetings of the NEJAC. He explained that each NEJAC meeting now will focus on a single issue and its relationship to environmental justice. Announcing that this meeting of the NEJAC would focus on permitting, Mr. Herman stated that through panel discussions, members of the NEJAC, EPA, and other meeting participants will examine aspects of permitting related to various authorities and opportunities where the agency can ensure that environmental justice is integrated into the decision-making process for issuing permits. Mr. Herman concluded his remarks by noting that numerous assistant administrators and other senior-level managers of EPA will be in attendance at this meeting.

Mr. Barry Hill, Director, EPA OEJ, began his remarks by stating that environmental justice is "something that belongs to everyone" in that every American citizen is entitled to clean air, water, and land based on the United States' protective environmental laws. He continued by defining environmental justice, and explaining that the concept:

▸ Acknowledges that environmental justice is a basic right of all Americans to live and work in environmentally protected surroundings.

▸ Recognizes that environmental justice is not only an environmental issue, but a public health issue.

▸ Recognizes that environmental justice is forward-looking and goal-oriented because the concept seeks to include affected communities in the decision-making processes.

▸ Indicates that environmental justice is inclusive.

Mr. Hill then stated that based on these premises the definition of environmental justice is compatible with the mission of EPA to protect human health and to safeguard the environment.

Continuing his remarks, Mr. Hill pointed out that environmental justice is at a critical stage from the point of view of environmental law and public policy. He then proceeded to provide historical examples of environmental justice, starting with the issuance in 1987 of a report by the United Church of Christ on race and environmental contamination to present day legal cases to highlight the various stages of environmental justice as a legal concept.

Mr. Hill concluded his remarks by stating that for this meeting OEJ has asked the NEJAC to provide advice and recommendations on how best to integrate environmental justice into the decision-making process related to permitting so that the concept can be applied as measurable, rationalized, and routine standards of evaluation.

Ms. Samantha Fairchild, Director, Office of Enforcement, Compliance, and Environmental Justice, EPA Region 3, emphasized that environmental justice continues to be a major area of concern at EPA Region

3 and that the regional office has taken steps to improve communication among all affected stakeholders. For example, she explained that EPA Region 3 is developing partnerships with state environmental agencies in the five-state region to provide assistance during the decision-making process related to permits. This effort includes establishing consistent meetings with states to discuss potential environmental justice issues before those issues become legal problems, she said. Ms. Fairchild also noted that EPA Region 3 has participated in Pennsylvania's Environmental Equity Work Group to define and identify criteria for environmental justice communities.

Continuing her remarks, Ms. Fairchild also noted that the regional office has been involved in several studies to investigate public health issues in environmental justice areas with heavy industry as well as conducted a study in a southwest Philadelphia, Pennsylvania area that is heavily concentrated with auto body and paint shops. She explained that the information collected from these studies will assist the state of Pennsylvania and Region 3 meet the needs of its citizens. Ms. Fairchild concluded her remarks by stating that the NEJAC is a valuable tool to grapple with the many complex problems facing communities related to environmental justice.

Mr. Bradley Campbell, White House Council on Environmental Quality (CEQ), reported on the second environmental justice listening session held in New York, New York in March 1999 that continued to bring together various federal agencies and community members to discuss issues related to environmental justice. Mr. Campbell explained that the purpose of the listening sessions was to ensure the environmental justice principles that have been integrated into EPA's policies and programs also are being implemented in other federal agencies actions that affect local communities. As a result of the listening session, he noted, several federal agencies, such as the U.S. Army Corps of Engineers (USACE), agreed to reopen public comment periods to review permits related to transportation decisions for New York City. In addition, the Healthcare Financing Administration agreed to help local New York communities to gain better access to medical care for asthma related health problems.

PUBLIC COMMENT PERIODS

The NEJAC hosted public comment periods on November 30 and December 1, 1999. More than 30 people participated in the two public comment periods. Significant concerns expressed during the public comment periods included:

▸   Several commenters continued to express concern about the "unfair process" under which permits are issued by the Louisiana Department of Environmental Quality (LDEQ).

▸   Many commenters expressed concern about the "unrealistic" time frame by which to review and provide comments on proposed permits during the decision-making process. Many commenters recommended that EPA revise the time line related to issuing a permit to provide for earlier notification of a proposed permit, as well as provide documents in easier to understand language.

▸   Several commenters expressed concern about the lack of options available for recourse once a permit has been issued and a facility has begun operations.

▸   Several commenters recommended that the NEJAC address environmental justice issues at federal facilities.

PANELS ON PERMITTING AND ENVIRONMENTAL JUSTICE

The NEJAC, in its continuing efforts to provide independent advice to the EPA Administrator on areas related to environmental justice, focused its fourteenth meeting on a specific policy issue -- permitting and environmental justice. On Tuesday, November 30, 1999, the members of the NEJAC listened to a series of panels comprised of various stakeholders that were designed to provide insight into the issues and concerns raised with respect to environmental justice in the permitting process.

Mr. Richard Lazarus, Professor of Law, Georgetown University Law Center and former member of the Enforcement Subcommittee of the NEJAC, provided background information on the historical development of integrating concerns related to environmental justice into the permitting process. Mr. Lazarus explained that "environmental justice permitting" refers to the consideration of concerns related to environmental justice in the context of an environmental permitting authority's decision to grant, deny, or condition a permit at a facility, the operation of which has adverse or potentially adverse environmental effects on the community. Ms. Zulene Mayfield, Chester Residents Concerned for Quality Living, presented an overview on the challenges her community has faced related to state environmental agencies and the permitting process. Ms. Mayfield emphasized the necessity for local and state agencies to allow local affected communities to participate earlier and more often in the decision-making process. Mr. Carlos Porras, Communities for a Better Environment, provided information on several communities near Los Angeles, California facing environmental justice issues related to air quality and permitting. Mr. Porras explained that there are several challenges EPA needs to address related to permitting that included collecting more reliable data.

The panel presentations included (Exhibit ES-2 provides the names of the panelists):

▸ *Facilitated Dialogue* — Mr. Kojo Nnamdi of National Public Radio, facilitated a dialogue among representatives of communities; industry; tribes; and state, local, and federal governments to identify issues and concerns related to environmental justice and permitting. (Exhibit ES-3 shows Mr. Nnamdi facilitating.) The primary issue identified by all stakeholder groups was that the public should become involved in the permitting process as early and as often as possible. Several members of the panel expressed concern that members of the public believe that public outreach related to permitting is superficial, citing the fact that although a regulation may take two years to develop, the public only receives 30 days in which to review and provide comment.

ES-3: Mr. Kojo Nnamdi facilitating a dialogue session on issues related to environmental justice and the permitting process.

▸ *EPA Panel* — Senior managers from EPA's Office of Solid Waste and Emergency Response (OSWER), Office of Air and Radiation (OAR), Office of Water (OW), and Region 3 provided information on their program's efforts to incorporate environmental justice into the permitting processes. Each of the headquarter program offices announced to the members of the NEJAC various commitments to increase public involvement and revise the permitting processes to integrate environmental justice into them.

PANEL PRESENTATIONS ON PERMITTING RELATED TO ENVIRONMENTAL JUSTICE

Overview:

Introduction:	Richard Lazarus, Georgetown University Law Center (Washington, D.C.)
Community Case Studies:	Zulene Mayfield, Chester Residents Concerned for Quality Living (Chester, Pennsylvania)
	Carlos Porras, Communities for a Better Environment (Los Angeles, California)

Facilitated Dialogue:

Community:	Margie Richard, Local Resident (Norco, Louisiana)
Community:	Zack Lyde, Local Pastor (Brunswick, Georgia)
Industry/Business:	Michael Steinberg, Morgan, Lewis and Bockius (Washington, D.C.)
Tribal/Indigenous:	Bill Swaney, Confederated Salish and Kootenai Tribes (Pablo, Montana)
State Government:	Alissa Harris, State of Pennsylvania (Harrisburg, Pennsylvania)
Local Government:	Matt Ward, National Association of Local Government Environmental Professionals (Washington, D.C.)
Federal Government:	William Harnett, U.S. Environmental Protection Agency (EPA), Office of Air Quality Planning and Standards (Washington, D.C.)

EPA Panel:

Office of Solid Waste and Emergency Response:	Timothy Fields, Jr., Assistant Administrator (AA)
Office of Air and Radiation:	Robert Brenner, Acting Deputy AA
Office of Water:	Dana Minerva, Deputy AA
Region 3:	John Armstead, Associate Director, Environmental Services Division

Panel 1: Addressing Real Life Dilemmas of Environmental Justice in Permitting: How Do We Respond to the Legacy of Land Use Impacts?

Academia:	Yale Rubin, Professor Emeritus, Massachusetts Institute of Technology (Cambridge, Massachusetts)
Industry/Business:	Michael Gerrand, Arnold & Porter (New York, New York)
Community:	Paula Forbis, Environmental Health Coalition (San Diego, California)
Local Government:	Sarah Lyles, City of Detroit (Detroit, Michigan)

Panel 2: The Current State of Environmental Justice and Permitting: What Are Its Limitations?

Industry/Business:	Jerry Martin, Dow Chemical (Midland, Michigan)
Community:	Larry Charles, O.N.E./C.H.A.N.E. (Hartford, Connecticut)
State Government:	Andrea Kreiner, Delaware Department of Natural Resources and Environmental Control (Dover, Delaware)
Federal Government:	Steve Heare, EPA Office of Solid Waste

Panel 3: Opportunities for Improvement: What Factors Should EPA Consider to Help Ensure Environmental Justice in Permitting?

Academia:	Eileen Gauna, Southwestern University Law School, (Los Angeles, California)
State Government:	Robert Shinn, New Jersey Department of Environmental Protection (Trenton, New Jersey)
Community:	Nathalie Walker, Earthjustice Legal Defense Fund (New Orleans, Louisiana)
Tribal/Indigenous:	Stuart Harris, Confederated Tribes of Umatilla (Pendleton, Oregon)

▸ *Panel 1: Addressing Real Life Dilemmas of Environmental Justice in Permitting: How Do We Respond to the Legacy of Land Use Impacts?* — Representatives from academia, industry, community, and local government discussed the dilemmas for the permitting process related to the historical development of land use and zoning requirements. Several members of the panel recommended that EPA involve stakeholders of local government earlier in the development of guidance and policy to help prepare local governments to implement new regulations.

▸ *Panel 2: The Current State of Environmental Justice and Permitting: What Are Its Limitations?* — This multi stakeholder panel identified areas of concern and gaps related to integrating environmental justice into the permitting process. A primary concern expressed by several members of the panel focused on the need for local, state, and federal government agencies to diversify their staff to better understand the needs and concerns of their constituents.

▸ *Panel 3: Opportunities for Improvement: What Factors Should EPA Consider to Help Ensure Environmental Justice in Permitting?* — Members of the multi stakeholder panel provided recommendations to EPA on how to improve efforts to integrate concerns related to environmental justice into the permitting process. Several key recommendations included:

  – Create an air emissions credits trading review board to evaluate the disparate effects the trading of air emissions credits may have on an affected community.

  – Provide additional resources to improve data from geographical information systems to more accurately identify demographics and other cultural considerations.

COMMON THEMES

During the meetings of the Executive Council and its subcommittees, the members of the NEJAC discussed a wide range of issues related to environmental justice. Specific concerns of and commitments made by the NEJAC include:

▸ Continued concern about the "crisis" environmental contamination conditions under which certain residents of Louisiana live.

▸ Concern about the lack of public participation in the decision-making process related to issuing permits.

▸ Recommendation that EPA develop a process by which the agency can step in to "fill the regulatory gap" left when EPA is not the primary authority.

Members of the NEJAC recommended that the EPA Administrator assume an active role in discussions with LDEQ about the environmental contamination and the issuance of permits in that state. In addition, the Executive Council also approved a resolution that requested that the EPA Administrator recommend that the Inspector General of EPA conduct an audit of the LDEQ to ensure that the state agency is in compliance with applicable environmental laws.

Members of the NEJAC, as well as members of the various panels, agreed that local communities need to be included often and as early as possible in the decision-making process related to issuing permits. The Executive Council agreed to create a special work group to develop a report to provide advice on how EPA can integrate concerns related to environmental justice into the permitting process in a manner that would be beneficial to all stakeholders. Ms. Vernice Miller-Travis, Partnership for Sustainable Brownfields Redevelopment and chair of the Waste and Facility Siting Subcommittee of the NEJAC, agreed to chair the work group.

Several members of the NEJAC expressed concern about several cases, such as waste transfer stations, in which a "regulatory gap" is created because EPA is not the primary authority and the local or state agency is not responding to concerns of its constituents. The members recommended that EPA develop a process by which the agency can step in to "fill" such a gap.

SUMMARIES OF THE SUBCOMMITTEE
MEETINGS

Summarized below are the deliberations of the members of the six subcommittees of the NEJAC during their meetings.

Air and Water Subcommittee

The Air and Water Subcommittee reviewed the activities of its three work groups on cumulative permitting, urban air toxics, and fish consumption, and proposed a new work group of the subcommittee which would focus on public utilities. Updates from the current work groups included:

▸   The Work Group on Cumulative Permitting proposed a list of issues for EPA to consider related to public participation and permitting.

▸   The Work Group on Urban Air Toxics discussed and offered comment to EPA OAR on the agency's urban air toxic strategy.

▸   The Work Group on Fish Consumption focused its efforts on subsistence fish consumption, specifically related to cultural practices of native communities; fish monitoring; the necessity for fish advisories; and reducing human exposure to contaminants in fish.

The subcommittee also hosted a joint session with the Enforcement Subcommittee of the NEJAC that focused on OAR's economic incentives program (EIP), Tier II/gasoline sulfur rule, and OW's proposed rule on standards for total maximum daily load (TMDL).

Enforcement Subcommittee

The members of the Enforcement Subcommittee heard three presentations on environmental justice and the decision-making process related to permitting. The members of the subcommittee also participated in a discussion about the proposed budget cuts for OECA. In addition, Ms. Ann Goode, Director, EPA Office of Civil Rights (OCR), provided the subcommittee with an update on activities at OCR and the progress on processing administrative complaints filed under Title VI of the Civil Rights Act of 1964 (Title VI).

In addition, the members of the subcommittee discussed at length three pending resolutions that had been forwarded by mail ballot vote to the Executive Council of the NEJAC for approval. The pending resolutions addressed state-issued variances from the Clean Air Act permit requirements, EPA's proposed guidance on EIP, and the economic benefit to industry of noncompliance with environmental laws. The members of the subcommittee also began discussions on a proposed resolution on concentrated animal feeding operations (CAFO).

Health and Research Subcommittee

Members of the Health and Research Subcommittee heard presentations by the following individuals:

▸   Dr. Dorothy Patton, EPA Office of Research and Development (ORD), presented information on the responsibilities of ORD, including the office's activities and new directions for the future.

▸   Dr. William Sanders, EPA Office of Pollution Prevention and Toxic Substances (OPPTS), provided an update on EPA's proposed lead rule, EPA's community-right-know program, and the agency's community assistance technical team.

▸ Dr. Henry Falk, Agency for Toxic Substances and Disease Registry (ASTDR), discussed his agency's approach to conducting environmental health assessments.

▸ Dr. Jerome Balter, Public Interest Law Center of Philadelphia, provided information on a model used by the city of Philadelphia, Pennsylvania to evaluate and support an administrative complaint filed under Title VI.

Members of the subcommittee also agreed to develop resolutions on 1) guidelines for community-based research ethics and 2) to request that EPA and other federal agencies explore opportunities to fund environmental health research topics identified by communities.

Indigenous Peoples Subcommittee

Members of the Indigenous Peoples Subcommittee continued to discuss the development of a consultation and collaboration guidance to provide assistance to federal and other agencies on how to participate in meaningful consultation with tribal governments and tribal communities. The subcommittee agreed to distribute the draft guidance to all federally recognized tribes for review and comment. In addition, the subcommittee agreed to forward by March 2000 a copy of the guidance to the members of the Executive Council for approval.

Members of the subcommittee also discussed and developed a strategic plan for the subcommittee for the next two years. Several goals express in the strategic plan include identifying key environmental justice issues, particularly related to permitting, in Indian Country and provide training to members of the NEJAC on environmental justice issues related to indigenous peoples.

In addition, members of the subcommittee discussed EPA's proposed core standards for water quality for Indian Country, the air permitting program related to tribes, and the recent trade negotiations related to persistent organic pollutants (POP).

International Subcommittee

Members of the International Subcommittee reviewed more than 100 recommendations that were generated from the Roundtable on Environmental Justice on the U.S./Mexico Border meeting held in August 1999 in San Diego, California. The members established priorities among the recommendations and decided to focus on:

▸ Creation of a binational community-based commission that would monitor and assist in the development of environmental policies that would affect the border region.

▸ Cleanup two contaminated sites, Metales y Derivados near Tijuana, Mexico and the Condado Prestos in Ciudad Juarez, Mexico.

▸ Conduct of a site assessment of the Matamoros Tamaulipas site in Mexico.

Members of the subcommittee also participated in discussions with Mr. Alan Hecht, Principal Deputy Assistant Administrator, EPA Office of International Activities (OIA); Mr. Gregg Cooke, Regional Administrator, EPA Region 6; and Dr. Clarice Gaylord, Special Assistant to the Regional Administrator, San Diego Border Liaison Office, EPA Region 9.

Waste and Facility Siting Subcommittee

Members of the Waste and Facility Siting Subcommittee discussed issues related to environmental justice and the administration of the Superfund program by EPA. The members of the subcommittee recommended that communities be protected as EPA continues to delegate authority to tribes and states under Superfund.

Members of the Waste Transfer Station Work Group of the subcommittee presented its report of recommendations on criteria for siting waste transfer stations, a planning process to assure a more equitable distribution of waste transfer facilities among communities, and a more deliberative approach to evaluate how many of these types of facilities are necessary. The members of the work group noted that, in the absence of a federal baseline for waste transfer stations, there exists an enormous variability in operating practices among such facilities.

In response to continued concerns expressed during earlier public comment periods of the NEJAC, members of the subcommittee agreed to participate in quarterly conference calls convened by EPA Region 6 to address environmental justice issues related to Calcasieu Parish, Louisiana. Also, members of the subcommittee agreed to address differences between presentations made by staff of EPA related to the relocation of community members of Pensacola, Florida and those comments offered by affected community members during the December 1, 1999 public comment period.

SUMMARY OF APPROVED RESOLUTIONS

This section summarizes resolutions that were discussed by the subcommittees and approved by the Executive Council of the NEJAC during the meeting. Appendix A provides the full text of each resolution that was approved by the Executive Council.

▸ The NEJAC recommends that EPA request that Puerto Rico Commonwealth revise its State Implementation Plan to comply with the .1lbs/MBTU federal emission limitation of particulate matter and the appropriate sulfur dioxide emission limitation for the entire island including the non-attainment area.

▸ The NEJAC recommends that EPA request that the U.S. Department of State and the United States Trade Representative (USTR) comply with the provisions expressed in Executive Order 12898 on environmental justice and Executive Order 13141 related to environmental reviews of trade agreements.

▸ The NEJAC recommends that EPA communicate to the U.S. Secretary of State that the United States supports the adoption of the current draft declaration on the rights of Indigenous Peoples before the United Nations.

▸ The NEJAC requests that EPA Region 2 facilitate a meeting between the Westside Homeowners Protective Association, the Venice Park Civic Association, the U.S. Department of Transportation, the South Jersey Transportation Authority, and the New Jersey Department of Environmental Protection to address the issues of exposure of community residents from contaminated soil, long-term air quality issues, and the potential adverse effects to the community residents after the construction of the Atlantic City/Brigantine Connector tunnel project.

▸ The NEJAC recommends that the EPA Administrator request that the Inspector General of EPA conduct a full audit of the state of Louisiana's permitting programs with particular attention to the violations of EPA's public participation regulations, the public participation guidelines of the NEJAC, and the provisions of the U.S. Constitution.

▸ The NEJAC recommends that EPA amend the agency's proposed EIP regulations to include considerations and requirements related to environmental justice.

▸ The NEJAC recommends that EPA's policies on determining appropriate penalties for noncompliance require that these penalties reflect the economic benefit of noncompliance enjoyed by violating facilities.

▸ The NEJAC recommends that EPA adopt a national policy which prohibits federal recognition of variances issued by states to the permitting requirements under Title V of the Clean Air Act.

NEXT MEETING

The next meeting of the NEJAC is scheduled for May 23 through 26, 2000 in Atlanta, Georgia at the Omni at CNN Center. Planned activities will include two opportunities for the public to offer comments. Exhibit ES-4 identifies the dates and locations of future meetings as well as the issues the NEJAC plans to address. For further information about this pending meeting visit NEJAC's home page on the Internet at: *http://www.epa.gov/oeca/main/ej/nejac/conf_ne.html* or call EPA's toll-free environmental justice hotline at 1-800-962-6215.

Exhibit ES-4

**FUTURE MEETINGS OF
THE NATIONAL ENVIRONMENTAL JUSTICE ADVISORY COUNCIL**

Date	Location	Issue
May 23 - 26, 2000	Atlanta, Georgia	Community Health
December 2000	Washington, D.C.	Interagency Environmental Justice Implementation

APPENDIX A
FULL TEXT OF THE RESOLUTIONS

RESOLUTION CALLING FOR AN AUDIT OF
LOUISIANA PERMITTING PROGRAMS

WHEREAS, public participation in environmental decision-making is fundamental to environmental justice, as it allows those affected by decisions to take part in them;

WHEREAS, all major environmental laws contain legally binding public participation requirements;

WHEREAS, EPA offices with permitting authority further agreed to and embraced the NEJAC Public Participation Guidelines;

WHEREAS, the right to legal representation is indispensable for public participation and essential to the viability of citizen suit provisions of said federal environmental laws;

WHEREAS, public participation and speech on environmental decisions is constitutionally protected by the 1st Amendment;

WHEREAS, NEJAC has heard testimony at each of its last five meetings from residents of Louisiana, who have presented substantial evidence indicating a pattern of intimidation by the State of Louisiana of citizens engaged in public comment, leading to the curtailing of citizens' right to free speech in environmental permitting processes;

WHEREAS, the State of Louisiana has moved to abridge citizens' rights to legal representation in environmental decision-making;

WHEREAS, the failure to guarantee public participation represents dereliction of the State of Louisiana's delegated and authorized environmental permitting programs;

WHEREAS, implementation failures and delegated programs undermine the federal government's authority for those programs at the national level;

WHEREAS, such threats to federal authority, if confirmed, provide grounds for the revocation of the State of Louisiana's permitting authorities;

THEREFORE, BE IT RESOLVED, that the NEJAC recommends that the Administrator direct the Inspector General to conduct a full audit of the State of Louisiana's permitting programs with particular attention to violations of the Agency's public participation regulations, the NEJAC's public participation guidelines, and the U.S. Constitution.

RESOLUTION ON POLLUTION CAUSED BY THE PUERTO RICO
ELECTRIC POWER AUTHORITY (PREPA)

WHEREAS, the Puerto Rico State Implementation Plan Revision of 1993 to reduce PM10 has failed to obtain attainment in the Guaynabo non attainment area

WHEREAS, NAAQS exceedances have occurred for four consecutive years

WHEREAS, these exceedances were predicted in the modeling process of the 1993 SIP revision

WHEREAS, exceedances in Puerto Rico during dust migration episodes from the Sahara dust and the Monserrate volcano eruptions are always predictable by the available satellite technology

WHEREAS, the state cannot control non anthropogenic emissions, it can control anthropogenic emissions from point sources such as power plants stacks to ensure NAAQS compliance

WHEREAS, the use of a fuel with a sulfur content of 1.5% as a control strategy to minimize the impact of the Puerto Rico Electric Power Authority (PREPA) in the non attainment area in Cata-Guaynabo has failed to obtain attainment in the area

WHEREAS, PREPA has no pollution control in its stacks

WHEREAS, a residual oil with 1.5% of sulfur content is considered a dirty fuel

WHEREAS, the particulate emission limitation (mass emission) of .3lbs/lbs/MBU is less restrictive than the federal standard of 0.1 lbs/MBTU

WHEREAS, the state mass emission standard of 0.3 lbs/MBTU has never been proven by the state to be equivalent to 20% opacity,

WHEREAS, the PR state mass emission limitation of .3lbs/MBTU has been identified by EQB officials as a "typographical error'

WHEREAS, the state emission standard cannot be less restrictive than the federal particulate standards,

WHEREAS, PREPA has been identified as egregious opacity violator while firing 1.5% sulfur fuels since 1993,

WHEREAS, the use of a fuel with 1.5% sulfur content has failed to sustain a clean emission in PREPA's stacks,

WHEREAS, relying in opacity as the only federally emission standard to protect the health of the people from excessive sulfur dioxide emissions from a dirty fuel results in an unequal protection of law to residents,

WHEREAS, PREPA has been convicted of criminal environmental actions in a federal Court as is under certain strict probation terms,

WHEREAS, eliminating the mass emission limitation in a non attainment area for particulates, in the Cataño-Guaynabo area, contravenes the Clean Air Act

WHEREAS, PREPA is the second Public Utility with the highest revenues in the USA,

WHEREAS, PREPA has a monopoly in energy sales, even in the presence of other cogenerators

WHEREAS, PREPA is included by EPA as one of the 100 dirtiest power plants in terms of sulfur dioxide and particulate emissions,

WHEREAS, the installment of appropriate enforceable limitations is the only mechanism available in Puerto Rico to protect its citizens from acid rain and sulfur dioxide emissions because PREPA is exempted to comply with the tittle IV program provisions

WHEREAS, PREPA has made significant modifications and capital investments and no longer qualifies to be exempted to comply with the New Source Performance Standards,

WHEREAS, Puerto Rico must be treated as a state,

Be it resolved that EPA should take the following actions,

1. To request the Puerto Rico Commonwealth State to revise its State Implementation Plan in order to establish the .1lbs/BMTU Federal emission limitation of particulate, and the appropriate sulfur dioxide emission limitation for the entire island including the non attainment area,

2. To request PREPA to establish a continuous SOx emission monitoring mechanism

3. To request PREPA to fire a residual oil with a sulfur content no higher than .5 percent in all of its plants.

RESOLUTION ON "CREDIBLE DETERRENCE" CIVIL PENALTIES: CAPTURING THE ECONOMIC BENEFIT OF NONCOMPLIANCE

Whereas, "Capturing the Economic Benefit" means that when a penalty is assessed against an environmental violator, a significant part of the assessment is calculating the costs avoided as a result of non-compliance, plus the interest earned on money as a result of delayed compliance; and

Whereas, Examples of economic benefit from noncompliance include delayed and avoided pollution control expenses, delayed and avoided installation, operation, and maintenance costs of pollution control equipment, and delayed and avoided costs of one-time acquisitions needed for compliance; and

Whereas, under U.S. EPA Policy and many federal environmental laws and regulations, one of the major considerations in calculation of any proposed penalty assigned to a violator is the question of what the economic benefit was to the violator; and

Whereas, the underlying policy consideration is that the penalty burden must be at least as great as the benefit of the violation or there would be no reason to comply; and

Whereas, the EPA Strategic Plan, Goal 9, calls for the Agency to provide a "credible deterrent to pollution and greater compliance with the law";

We hereby resolve that:

▸ EPA Penalty Policy which requires that penalties should include the component of economic benefit should be complied with at the national, regional, and state level.

▸ Technical assistance in calculating the economic benefit (EBN calculation training) should be provided to all enforcement authorities who assert that they can't do it because they don't know how.

▸ A model penalty policy that includes providing for the calculation of economic benefit should be made available to all enforcement authorities who assert that they can't do it because they don't have such a penalty policy.

▸ Any enforcement authority asserting that their laws prevent them from calculating the economic benefit should be required to provide an Attorney General's (or the equivalent) certification to that effect.

▸ EPA Regional Officials should consider taking independent enforcement actions against facilities in cases where state assessed penalties do not recover substantial economic benefits of noncompliance.

▸ A requirement of capturing the economic benefit should be incorporated as part of the Memoranda of Agreement with the Regions, or EPA's Performance Partnership Agreements with the delegated agencies, or through any other delegation agreements.

▸ To establish credible deterrence it should be made clear that agencies are delegated legal authority to establish general pollution control requirements consistent with federal statutory mandates and EPA policies and that as to capturing the economic benefit, they will not be allowed to sink below the minimum.

RESOLUTION ON EPA TO AMEND ITS ECONOMIC INCENTIVE PROGRAM (EIP) REGULATIONS TO INCLUDE ENVIRONMENTAL JUSTICE CONSIDERATIONS AND REQUIREMENTS

WHEREAS, the EPA is advocating both environmental justice as a means to reduce pollution in communities of color and pollution trading as a cost-effective method to reduce pollution.

WHEREAS, the EPA has adopted Economic Incentive Program (EIP) regulations which establish approvability requirements for pollution trading programs.

WHEREAS, the EIP regulations currently do not include safeguards <u>sufficient</u> to prevent adverse environmental justice impacts, including the creation of toxic hot spots in communities of color.

WHEREAS, the Assistant Administrator of the Office of Air and Radiation (OAR) has met with the NEJAC Enforcement Subcommittee to discuss environmental justice concerns related to emissions trading, and appeared generally receptive to the concerns raised by the NEJAC.

WHEREAS, the NEJAC recognizes the willingness of EPA OAR to continue to have a dialogue with the NEJAC until these issues are resolved.

WHEREAS, certain pollution trading programs have the potential to create, perpetuate or exacerbate air pollution toxic hot spots in communities of color by allowing facilities in those communities to increase or continue emissions.

WHEREAS, certain pollution trading programs allow facilities to increase or continue emissions of highly toxic chemicals, due to offsets obtained from decreases in less toxic chemical emissions, thereby resulting in a net increase in airborne toxicity.

WHEREAS, since stationary source polluters are <u>often disproportionately located in communities</u> of color, while mobile source pollution is widely distributed geographically, mobile to stationary source pollution trading has the potential to create or exacerbate toxic hot sports.

WHEREAS, pollution trading programs require accurate quantification of emissions reduced and increased through the program, and such quantification is particularly difficult in the case of mobile source trading programs.

WHEREAS, pollution credits should only be granted for emission reductions that are real, surplus, and quanitifiable, and pollution credits should therefore not be granted for emission reductions that would have resulted even in the absence of the pollution trading program.

WHEREAS, economic modeling tools exist that allow agencies to predict the probable geographic and demographic impact of pollution trading programs, including the location of probable pollution credit purchasers and sellers.

WHEREAS, a fundamental principle of the environmental justice movement is that communities affected by pollution must be allowed to participate in decisions affecting their environment.

BE IT RESOLVED THAT NEJAC urges EPA to Amend the EIP Regulations to:

▸ Prohibit the trading of toxic air pollutants, as defined in the Emergency Planning and Community Right-to-Know Act <u>if the result would be adverse health or environmental impact(s) in an environmental justice community, and unless EPA requires the states to develop adequate quantification protocols that must be reviewed and approved by EPA into an enforceable state implementation plan (SIP) prior to trading plan implementation to ensure accurate quantification of pollutants to be traded and to ensure enforceability and verifiability.</u>

▸ If trading of toxic chemicals is allowed, prohibit emissions trading that will result in an increase in toxic chemical pollution in already overburdened communities, taking into account cumulative pollution risks. <u>If trading of toxic chemicals is allowed, require implementing agency to consider selective toxicity of specific chemicals being traded, and to prohibit trading that will expose the public to unacceptable risk.</u>

▸ Prior to approval of any pollution trading program, require the agency proposing the program to conduct an economic analysis ~~similar~~ comparable to the model prepared by the Regional Economic Modeling, Inc. (REMI) to determine the location of probable emission credit purchasers and sellers. Require the agency to overlay the REMI analysis with demographic information to determine whether the proposed trading program will have an adverse impact on communities of color. Prohibit emissions trading programs that are predicted to have an adverse impact on communities of color.

A-4

- Require that at a minimum, all facilities ~~must~~ install technology-based controls defined as reasonably available control technology (RACT) under the Clean Air Act, and prohibit trading that allows companies to avoid installing RACT.

- Require all emissions trading programs to incorporate public participation components that include notification to affected communities of any trade that will result in an increase or continuation of toxic chemical pollution, and allow the affected communities a reasonable opportunity to review and comment upon said adverse impacts. Require the responsible agency to retain discretion to revise or reject the proposed pollution trade based upon comments received.

- Prohibit mobile-to-stationary source trading where the result would be adverse health or environmental impact(s) in an environmental justice community, and unless EPA requires the states to develop adequate quantification protocols that must be reviewed and approved by EPA into an enforceable state implementation plan (SIP) prior to trading plan implementation to ensure accurate quantification of pollutants to be traded and to ensure enforceability and verifiability.

- EPA should retain requirements in found in the emissions trading policy statement regulation requiring a portion of the economic benefit resulting from pollution trading to benefit the public through increased emission reductions.

RESOLUTION ON EPA TO ADOPT A NATIONAL POLICY PROHIBITING FEDERAL RECOGNITION OF STATE-ISSUED VARIANCES

WHEREAS, the Region IX of the EPA is considering whether to grant federal recognition of state-issued variances from Title V permit requirements, and has proposed to recognize such variances in cases of malfunction, start-up, shut-down, and maintenance;

WHEREAS, the federal recognition of these variances would preclude both federal and community enforcement of the federal Clean Air Act where violations have been documented, and thus provide a disincentive to compliance with Clean Air Act requirements;

WHEREAS, since stationary source polluters are disproportionately located in communities of color, issuance of variances to stationary sources will result in a disproportionate impact on these communities;

WHEREAS, the issuance of variances can result in increased impacts to public health from emissions of air toxics at levels above permit requirements and above those levels which have been analyzed for their impact to public health;

WHEREAS, the issuance of variances could impede reasonable further progress on attainment of federal air quality standards;

WHEREAS, Clean Air Act case law only allows for permit modifications after amendment to the appropriate State Implementation Plan;

WHEREAS, EPA enforcement policy takes into consideration problems such as malfunction, start-up, and shutdown procedures as mitigating factors to penalties assessed for violations;

NOW THEREFORE BE IT RESOLVED THAT:

NEJAC urges EPA to adopt a national policy which:

- Prohibits federal recognition of variances from Clean Air Act requirements, except for variances resulting in more stringent levels of control at the facility;

- Acknowledges that existing federal enforcement policies consider the nature of a violation and factors such as malfunction, start-up, shut-down, and maintenance as mitigating factors in determining the appropriate federal enforcement response.

- Requires consultation with NEJAC before consideration or approving any variance policy, by EPA or any of its regions.

RESOLUTION ON THE UNITED NATIONS DRAFT DECLARATION ON THE RIGHTS OF INDIGENOUS PEOPLES

WHEREAS Executive Order 12898 establishing the National Environmental Justice Advisory Council (NEJAC) recognizes that Indigenous Peoples as a group are especially vulnerable to disproportionate impacts of environmental despoliation;

WHEREAS Executive Order 13107 of December 15, 1998, requires all Executive Departments and Agencies to respect United States human rights international obligations relevant to their functions, and to perform such functions so as to respect and implement those obligations fully;

WHEREAS the International Covenant on Civil and Political Rights (ICCPR) is an international human rights obligation of the United States, which recognizes the right of all Peoples to Self-Determination, including the right of Peoples to freely pursue their economic, social and cultural development and to freely dispose of their natural wealth and resources;

WHEREAS, the ICCPR also provides that Peoples may not be deprived of their own means of subsistence;

WHEREAS, The Vienna Declaration and Program of Action, also applicable to the United States:

- Reaffirmed that all human rights are universal, indivisible, interdependent and interrelated;

- Reaffirmed the commitment of the International Community to ensure the enjoyment of all human rights and fundamental freedoms of Indigenous Peoples and to respect and value the diversity of their cultures and identities;

- Considered the denial of the right of self determination as a violation of human rights and underlined the importance of the effective realization of this right;

- Called for concerted, positive steps from the international community to ensure respect for all human rights of Indigenous Peoples on the basis of equality and non-discrimination, recognizing the value of their distinct identities, cultures and social organization;

WHEREAS, the international community has recognized the spiritual relationship between Indigenous Peoples and their lands and territories, notably through International Labor Organization Convention no. 169 and numerous special studies;

WHEREAS, other United Nations studies have found that Indigenous lands are being subjected to unprecedented development and frequently resultant irreparable environmental damage;

WHEREAS, the Right to Development is a right of Peoples in which the enjoyment of self determination and full sovereignty over all natural wealth and resources is fundamental;

WHEREAS, the United Nations Commission on Human Rights is presently considering a Draft declaration on the rights of Indigenous Peoples;

WHEREAS, the present draft of the declaration before the Human Rights Commission was elaborated with the full and ample participation of hundreds of Indigenous Nations and thousands of their representatives before the United Nations Working Group on Indigenous Populations over a 12 year period;

WHEREAS, recognizing and underscoring, that these Indigenous participants found that the present draft before the Commission on Human Rights is a minimal standard to ensure the survival of Indigenous Peoples and their environment;

WHEREAS, the human rights and fundamental freedoms recognized in the present draft of the UN declaration on the rights of Indigenous Peoples are universal, interdependent, indivisible and interrelated to the achievement of Environmental Justice for Indigenous Peoples;

WHEREAS, recognition and observance of the right of Self Determination is a necessary element of Environmental Justice for Indigenous Peoples, and further, is a pre-requisite for their enjoyment of all other human rights;

WHEREAS, the NEJAC recognizes that the United Nations Draft declaration on the rights of indigenous peoples as an urgent Environmental Justice issue for Indigenous Peoples in the United States;

BE IT RESOLVED:

• That NEJAC request the EPA Administrator to immediately communicate to the Secretary of State that the United States support the adoption of the present draft declaration on the rights of Indigenous Peoples before the United Nations, as presented by the Working Group on Indigenous Populations, without change or amendment, as an urgent Environmental Justice concern; and,

• That EPA and the Administrator request a timely response to her communication from the Secretary of State, to be transmitted in full to NEJAC and its Subcommittees.

RESOLUTION TO URGE EPA TO REQUEST THAT THE SECRETARY OF STATE AND THE UNITED STATES TRADE REPRESENTATIVE COMPLY WITH THE PROVISIONS OF EXECUTIVE ORDER 12898 AND THAT THEY PROVIDE ASSISTANCE IN ADDRESSING ENVIRONMENTAL JUSTICE ISSUES RAISING TRANSBOUNDARY AND INTERNATIONAL ISSUES

WHEREAS, Presidential Executive Order 12898, entitled "Federal Actions to Address Environmental Justice in Minority Populations and Low-Income Populations," directs that "each Federal agency shall make achieving environmental justice part of its mission by identifying and addressing, as appropriate, disproportionately high and adverse human health or environmental effects of its programs, policies, and activities on minority populations and low-income populations in the United States and its territories and possessions, the District of Columbia, the Commonwealth of Puerto Rico, and the Commonwealth of Mariana Islands;" and

WHEREAS, some international border areas, including areas of the U.S./Mexico border, are heavily populated on both sides of the border; and

WHEREAS, victims of disproportionate pollution impacts and environmental injustice resulting from international trade and commerce along the border area include American citizen people of color, poor people, Indigenous Peoples as well as other residents of the United States; and

WHEREAS, public comments and discussions at a recent "Roundtable on Environmental Justice Issues on the U.S./Mexico Border" (Border Roundtable), sponsored by the NEJAC International Subcommittee and EPA in San Diego, California (April 19-21), have made clear that there are significant pollution and other environmental issues affecting low-income, minority, and indigenous populations along the U.S./Mexico border area; and

WHEREAS, the political disenfranchisement of and environmental burdens on low-income, minority, and indigenous populations residing in border areas, such as the U.S./Mexico border region, are exacerbated by the lack of political and legal accountability of polluting facilities located outside of the United States; and

WHEREAS, Executive Order 12898 does not specifically mention the State Department and the U.S. Trade Representative's Office as Federal agencies within the scope of the Executive Order; and,

WHEREAS, some of the potential impacts of programs, policies, and activities of the State Department and the U.S. Trade Representative's Office clearly fall within the scope of the activities that Executive Order 12898 was intended and designed to address; and

WHEREAS, Executive order 13141 entitled Environmental Review of Trade Agreements, specifically calls for careful assessment and consideration of the environmental impacts of trade agreements such as those disproportionate impacts contemplated by Executive Order 12898; and,

WHEREAS, Executive Order 13141 requires environmental reviews and public comment on the environmental impacts of trade agreements in the United States, and where appropriate and prudent, on global and transboundary impacts; and,

WHEREAS, the NEJAC believes that it is imperative for all agencies whose programs, policies, and activities with a potential impact on low-income, minority, and indigenous populations engage in discussions about and substantively work on efforts to achieve the President's expressed goal of promoting environmental justice for such populations; and

WHEREAS, the State Department and the U.S. Trade Representative's Office can incorporate environmental justice concerns into their missions through existing environmental and human rights offices;

NOW THEREFORE BE IT RESOLVED THAT:

NEJAC urges the EPA Administrator to:

▸ Request that the Secretary of State and the United States Trade Representative comply with and further the provisions of and policies expressed in Executive Order 12898 and Executive Order 13141; and

▸ Request participation, in accordance with the provisions of Executive Order 12898, by the Secretary of State and the United States Trade Representative in the Interagency Working Group on Environmental Justice; and

▸ Request the Secretary of State and the United States Trade Representative to prepare an Environmental Justice Strategy, in accordance with the provisions of Executive Order 12898; and

▸ Seek designation by the President, in accordance with Sections 1-102 and 6-604 of Executive Order 12898, of the State Department and the United States Trade Representative's Office as agencies participating in the Interagency Working Group under Executive Order 12898 and covered by its provisions; and

▸ Develop, in cooperation with the Secretary of State, the United States Trade Representative, and the Council for Environmental Quality, criteria and methodologies for considering the transboundary environmental impacts on racial minority, low-income, and indigenous populations in the areas covered by Executive Order 12898 by the international activities of Federal agencies, including negotiation of international trade and other agreements.

▸ Request assistance from the Secretary of State in resolving concerns, such as the ones raised by various community organizations at the "Roundtable on Environmental Justice on the U.S./Mexico Border" (August 19-21, 1999, San Diego, California), concerning environmental degradation and pollution at the border as well as transboundary impacts of pollution.

RESOLUTION TO ADDRESS COMMUNITIES AT RISK FROM THE ATLANTIC CITY/ BRIGANTINE CONNECTOR TUNNEL PROJECT, ATLANTIC CITY, NEW JERSEY

WHEREAS, South Jersey Transportation Authority, in conjunction with the New Jersey Department of Transportation is constructing the Atlantic City/Brigantine Connector Tunnel.

WHEREAS, the Atlantic City Tunnel, will *bisect* the Atlantic City communities of the First Ward, Second Ward, Third Ward, Fourth Ward, and Venice Park area of Atlantic City, all of which consists of predominantly African-American residents.

WHEREAS, the Atlantic City Tunnel route has resulted in the relocation and displacement of homeowners that resided on the selected route.

WHEREAS, the Atlantic City Tunnel route traverses within 25 feet of the remaining residents.

WHEREAS, soils that will be excavated for the construction of the Atlantic City Tunnel are contaminated with heavy metals, petroleum-related compounds, and other organic and inorganic substances at levels in excess of health-based standards established by the New Jersey Department of Environmental Protection and 152,000 cubic yards of these soils will be reuse on site.

WHEREAS, the South Jersey Transportation Authority has rejected the request of community residents for controls ensure that contaminants in the soils do not migrate to the adjacent communities, such as air monitoring – on-site and off-site – of the contaminants found in the soils, continuous engineering controls, and covering of the soils.

WHEREAS, excavation of has continued for 9 months and community residents have begun to complain of respiratory difficulties since the beginning of construction – including the triggering of dormant asthma.

WHEREAS, analysis performed by South Jersey Transportation Authority and the New Jersey Department of Transportation acknowledge the possibility that there could be hot spots of carbon monoxide, particulates and sulfur dioxide in areas adjacent to the tunnel.

WHEREAS, the South Jersey Transportation Authority and the New Jersey Department of Transportation have rejected the request of community residents to install air control devices to address the emissions from vehicles using the tunnel and air monitoring of the emissions for a short time period after the tunnel is constructed to ensure local air quality does not create risk to the adjacent communities.

WHEREAS, South Jersey Transportation Authority has failed to address numerous other issues identified by community residents, including the potential for flooding, safety, and structural damage to homes.

WHEREAS, the Atlantic City Tunnel is funded by the State of New Jersey, administered by one of its agencies, and is to serve a casino that is supported by and would directly benefit the City of Atlantic City and the State of New Jersey.

WHEREAS, the unresponsiveness by all state agencies requires the intervention by the USEPA to prevent irreversible damage to health of community residents and the local communities.

THEREFORE BE IT RESOLVED, that the National Environmental Justice Advisory Council calls upon USEPA to IMMEDIATELY, through its Region II Offices, facilitate the convening of all parties, including the South Jersey Transportation Authority, New Jersey Department of Environmental Protection, and the New Jersey Department of Transportation, to address the immediate issues of exposure of community residents to contaminated soil during construction activities, and other issues of potential impact to the community residents after construction, such as flooding, and safety.

BE IT FURTHER RESOLVED, that the National Environmental Justice Advisory Council calls upon USEPA, in consultation with the US Department of Transportation, to convene a meeting of NJ Department of Transportation and South Jersey Transportation Authority, to address the long term air quality issues associated with tunnel.

APPENDIX B
LIST OF PARTICIPANTS

Marilyn Ababio
326 Pagosa Court
Palmdar, CA 93551
Phone: 661-273-7874
Fax: 661-273-0593
E-mail: marabio@aol.com

Julian Agyeman
Editor
Department of Urban and Environmental Policy
Tufts University
Local Environment
97 Talbot Avenue
Medford, MA 02155
Phone: 617-627-3394
Fax: 617-627-3377
E-mail: julian.agyeman@tufts.edu

LaVern Ajanaku
Environmental Justice Coordinator
Georgia Environmental Protection Division
205 Butler Street, SE, Suite 1162
Atlanta, GA 30334
Phone: 404-657-8688
Fax: 404-651-9425
E-mail: lavern_1ajanku@mail.dnr.state.ga.us

Rich Albores
Counsel
Environmental Appeals Board
U.S. Environmental Protection Agency
1200 Pennsylvania Avenue, NW, (MC 1103b)
Washington, DC 20460
Phone: 202-501-7060
Fax: 202-501-7580
E-mail: albores.richard@epamail.epa.gov

Mustafa Ali
Office of Environmental Justice
Office of Enforcement and Compliance Assurance
U.S. Environmental Protection Agency
1200 Pennsylvania Avenue, NW, (MC 2201A)
Washington, DC 20460
Phone: 202-564-2606
Fax: 202-501-0740
E-mail: ali.mustafa@epa.gov

Mike Allen
Office of General Counsel
U.S. Environmental Protection Agency
1200 Pennsylvania Avenue, NW, (MC 2313A)
Washington, DC 20460
Phone: 202-564-5404
Fax: 202-564-5412
E-mail: allen.mike@epa.gov

John Alter
Office of Prevention, Pesticides, and Toxic Substances
U.S. Environmental Protection Agency
1200 Pennsylvania Avenue, NW, (MC 7404)
Washington, DC 20460
Phone: 202-260-4315
Fax: 202-260-1096
E-mail: alter.john@epa.gov

Don Aragon
Executive Director
Wind River Environmental Quality Commission
Shoshone and Northern Arapaho Tribes
P.O. Box 217
Fort Washakie, WY 82514
Phone: 307-332-3164
Fax: 307-332-7579
E-mail: wreqc-twe@wyoming.com

Thomas M. Armitage
Engineering and Analysis Division
Office of Water
U.S. Environmental Protection Agency
1200 Pennsylvania Avenue, NW, (MC 4305)
Washington, DC 20460
Phone: 202-260-5388
Fax: 202-260-9380
E-mail: armitage.thomas@epa.gov

John A. Armstead
Associate Director
Environmental Services Division
Region 3
U.S. Environmental Protection Agency
1650 Arch Street
Philadelphia, PA 19103-2029
Phone: 215-814-3127
Fax: 215-814-2782
E-mail: armstead.john@epamail.epa.gov

Warren Arthur
Environmental Justice Coordinator
Region 6
U.S. Environmental Protection Agency
1445 Ross Avenue
Dallas, TX 76133
Phone: 214-665-8504
Fax: 214-665-7264
E-mail: arthur.warren@epa.gov

Michele Aston
Office of Reinvention Policy
Office of the Administrator
U.S. Environmental Protection Agency
1200 Pennsylvania Avenue, NW, (MC 1803)
Washington, DC 20460
Phone: 202-260-8767
Fax: 202-260-1812
E-mail: aston.michele@epa.gov

Shirley Augurson
Region 6
U.S. Environmental Protection Agency
1445 Ross Avenue, (6RA-DJ)
Dallas, TX 75202-2733
Phone: 214-665-7401
Fax: 214-665-7446
E-mail: augurson.shirley@epa.gov

Rose M. Augustine
President
Tucsonans For A Clean Environment
7051 W. Bopp Road
Tucson, AZ 85735-8621
Phone: 602-883-8424
Fax: Not Provided
E-mail: Not Provided

Cecil C. Bailey
Program Analyst
Environmental Justice Grants
Region 7
U.S. Environmental Protection Agency
901 North 5th Street
Kansas City, MO 66101
Phone: 913-551-7462
Fax: 913-551-7941
E-mail: bailey.cecil@epa.gov

Kathleen Bailey
Senior Management Analyst
Office of the Administrator
U.S. Environmental Protection Agency
1200 Pennsylvania Avenue, NW, (MC 1801)
Washington, DC 20460
Phone: 202-260-3413
Fax: 202-401-2474
E-mail: bailey.kathleen@epa.gov

Bev Baker
Environmental Scientist
CBPO
U.S. Environmental Protection Agency
410 Severn Avenue, Suite 109
Annapolis, MD 20912
Phone: 410-267-5772
Fax: 410-267-5777
E-mail: baker.beverly@epamail.epa.gov

Olivia Balandran
Regional Administrators Office
Region 6
U.S. Environmental Protection Agency
1445 Ross Avenue, (6RA-DJ)
Dallas, TX 75202-2733
Phone: 214-665-7257
Fax: 214-665-6648
E-mail: Not Provided

Fannie Ball
Score
109 Houston Avenue
Oak Ridge, TN 37830
Phone: 423-483-6073
Fax: Not Provided
E-mail: Not Provided

Jerome Balter
Public Interest Law Center of Philadelphia
125 south Ninth Street
Philadelphia, PA 19107
Phone: 215-627-7100
Fax: 215-627-3183
E-mail: Not Provided

Elvie Barlow
Environmental Scientist
Environmental Justice/Community Liaison
Program
Region 4
U.S. Environmental Protection Agency
61 Forsyth Street, SW
Atlanta, GA 30303-8960
Phone: 404-562-9650
Fax: 404-562-9664
E-mail: barlow.elvie@epa.gov

Elaine Barron
Paso del Norte Air Quality Task Force
1717 Brown Street, Bldg. 1-A
El Paso, TX 79912
Phone: 915-533-3566
Fax: 915-533-6102
E-mail: embarronmd@usa.net

Elizabeth Bartlett
Region 4
U.S. Environmental Protection Agency
61 Forsyth Street, NW
Atlanta, GA 30303
Phone: 404-562-9122
Fax: 404-562-9095
E-mail: bartlett.elizabeth@epa.gov

Rolando Bascumbe
Associate Regional Counsel
Region 4
U.S. Environmental Protection Agency
61 Forsyth Street, SW
Atlanta, GA 30303-8960
Phone: Not Provided
Fax: Not Provided
E-mail: Not Provided

Sharon Beard
Industrial Hygienist
Worker Education and Training Program
National Institute of Environmental Health
Sciences
U.S. Department of Health and Human
Services
P.O. Box 12233, (MD EC-25)
Research Triangle Park, NC 27709-2233
Phone: 919-541-1863
Fax: 919-558-7049
E-mail: beard1@niehs.nih.gov

Dwayne Beavers
Program Manager
Office of Environmental Services
Cherokee Nation
P.O. Box 948
Tahlequah, OK 74465-0671
Phone: 918-458-5496
Fax: 918-458-5499
E-mail: Not Provided

Jay Benforado
Deputy Associate Administrator
Office of Policy, Economics, and Innovation
Office of Policy
U.S. Environmental Protection Agency
1200 Pennsylvania Avenue, NW
Washington, DC 20460
Phone: 202-260-4332
Fax: 202-260-1812
E-mail: Not Provided

Kent Benjamin
Program Analyst
Outreach and Special Projects Staff
Office of Solid Waste and Emergency
Response
U.S. Environmental Protection Agency
1200 Pennsylvania Avenue, NW, (MC 5101)
Washington, DC 20460
Phone: 202-260-2822
Fax: 202-260-6606
E-mail: benjamin.kent@epa.gov

Pamela Bingham
Research Engineer
Bingham Consulting Services
P.O. Box 8248
Silver Spring, MD 20907
Phone: 202-260-6451
Fax: 202-401-9710
E-mail: bingham_engrsvs@hotmail.com

Debbie Bishop
Office of International Activities
U.S. Environmental Protection Agency
1200 Pennsylvania Avenue, NW
Washington, DC 20640
Phone: 202-564-6437
Fax: 202-565-5412
E-mail: bishop.debbie@epa.gov

Shelly Blake
Office Manager
Office of Environmental Justice
Office of Enforcement and Compliance
Assurance
U.S. Environmental Protection Agency
1200 Pennsylvania Avenue, NW, (MC 2201A)
Washington, DC 20004
Phone: 202-564-2633
Fax: 202-501-1079
E-mail: blake.shelley@epamail.epa.gov

Gale Bonanno
Special Assistant
Office of Environmental Compliance
Office of Enforcement and Compliance
Assurance
U.S. Environmental Protection Agency
1200 Pennsylvania Avenue, NW, (MC 2201A)
Washington, DC 20460
Phone: 202-564-2243
Fax: Not Provided
E-mail: Not Provided

Robert W. Bookman
Region 4
U.S. Environmental Protection Agency
61 Forsyth Street, SW
Atlanta, GA 30303
Phone: 404-562-9169
Fax: 404-562-9164
E-mail: bookman.robert@epamail.epa.gov

Frank Bove
Agency for Toxic Substances and Disease
Registry
1600 Clifton Road, NE Mailstop E-31
Atlanta, GA 30333
Phone: (404)639-5126
Fax: (404) 639-6219
E-mail: fjb0@cdc.gov

Gina Bowler
Program Analyst
Office of Solid Waste and Emergency
Response
U.S. Environmental Protection Agency
1200 Pennsylvania Avenue, NW, (MC 5304W)
Washington, DC 20460
Phone: 202-308-7279
Fax: 703-308-0522
E-mail: bowler.gina@epa.gov

Doris Bradshaw
Defense Depot Memphis Tennessee
Concerned Citizens Committee
1458 East Mallory Avenue
Memphis, TN 38106
Phone: 901-942-0329
Fax: 901-942-0800
E-mail: ddmtccc411@aol.com

Kenneth Bradshaw
Program Director
Defense Depot Memphis Tennessee
Concerned Citizens Committee
1458 East Mallory Avenue
Memphis, TN 38106
Phone: 901-942-0329
Fax: 901-942-0800
E-mail: ddmtccc411@aol.com

Jose T. Bravo
Southwest Network for Environmental and
Economic Justice
1066 Larwood Road
San Diego, CA 92114
Phone: 619-461-5011
Fax: 619-461-5011
E-mail: tonali@pacbell.net

Marc Brenman
Senior Policy Advisor
Departmental Office of Civil Rights
Office of the Secretary
U.S. Department of Transportation
400 7th Street, SW
Room 10217, S-30
Washington, DC 20590
Phone: 202-366-1119
Fax: 202-366-9371
E-mail: marc.brenman@ost.dot.gov

Robert Brenner
Deputy Assistant Administrator
Office of Air and Radiation
U.S. Environmental Protection Agency
1200 Pennsylvania Avenue, NW, (MC AR443)
Washington, DC 20460
Phone: 202-564-1668
Fax: 202-505-0394
E-mail: brenner.robert@epa.gov

Sue Briggum
Director
Governmental Affairs
Waste Management, Inc.
601 Pennsylvania Avenue, NW
North Building #300
Washington, DC 20004
Phone: 202-628-3500
Fax: 202-628-0400
E-mail: sue_briggum@wastemanagement.com

Jeanette Brown
Director
Small Business Administration
U.S. Environmental Protection Agency
1200 Pennsylvania Avenue, NW
Washington, DC 20460
Phone: 202-564-4100
Fax: Not Provided
E-mail: brown.jeanette@epa.gov

Rosalind Brown
Chief
Office of Customer Services
Region 4
U.S. Environmental Protection Agency
61 Forsyth Street, SW
Atlanta, GA 30303-3104
Phone: 404-562-8633
Fax: 404-562-8628
E-mail: brown.rosalind@epa.gov

Carol Browner
Administrator
Office of the Administrator
U.S. Environmental Protection Agency
1200 Pennsylvania Avenue, NW, (MC 1101)
Washington, DC 20460
Phone: 202-260-4700
Fax: Not Provided
E-mail: Not Provided

Mark Brownstein
Public Service Enterprise Group
Address Not Provided

Phone: Not Provided
Fax: Not Provided
E-mail: Not Provided

Bunyan Bryant
Professor
School of Natural Resources and Environment
University of Michigan
430 East University, Dana Building
Ann Arbor, MI 48109-1115
Phone: 734-769-4493
Fax: 734-763-2470
E-mail: bbryant@umich.edu

Lakeisha Bryant
Attorney/Advisor
U.S. Environmental Protection Agency
1200 Pennsylvania Avenue, NW
Washington, DC
Phone: 202-564-5616
Fax: 202-564-5442
E-mail: bryant.lakeisha@epa.gov

Marjorie Bucholtz
Brownfields Team Leader
Outreach and Special Projects Staff
Office of Solid Waste and Emergency
Response
U.S. Environmental Protection Agency
1200 Pennsylvania Avenue, NW, (MC 5103)
Washington, DC 20460
Phone: 202-260-9605
Fax: 202-960-6754
E-mail: Not Provided

Jan Buhrmann
Environmental Justice Program
Region 8
U.S. Environmental Protection Agency
999 18th Street, Suite 500
Denver, CO 80202
Phone: 303-312-6557
Fax: 303-312-6409
E-mail: buhrmann.jan@epa.gov

William Burkhart
Manager, Environmental Government
Relations
The Procter & Gamble Company
11310 Cornell Park Drive
Cincinnati, OH 45242
Phone: 513-626-4411
Fax: 513-626-1678
E-mail: burkhart.wt@pg.com

Alice Cage
NBRE Member
NBRE
525 Rafe Meyer Road
Baton Rouge, LA 70807
Phone: 225-775-6554
Fax: Not Provided
E-mail: Not Provided

Mike Callahan
U.S. Environmental Protection Agency
1200 Pennsylvania Avenue, NW, (MC P623-D)
Washington, DC 20460
Phone: 202-564-320
Fax: 202-565-0077
E-mail: callahan.michael@epa.gov

Barry K. Campbell
The EOP Group Incorporated
819 Seventh Street, NW, Suite 400
Washington, DC 20001
Phone: 202-833-8940
Fax: 202-833-8945
E-mail: bkcampbell@819eagle.com

Bradley Campbell
Associate Director
White House Council on Environmental Quality
722 Jackson Place, NW
Washington, DC 20503
Phone: 202-395-5750
Fax: 202-456-0753
E-mail: Not Provided

Pat Carey
Office of Solid Waste and Emergency
Response
U.S. Environmental Protection Agency
1200 Pennsylvania Avenue, NW
Washington, DC 20460
Phone: 703-603-8772
Fax: 703-603-9100
E-mail: carey.pat.epa.gov

Connie Carr
Region 3
U.S. Environmental Protection Agency
1650 Arch Street
Philadelphia, PA 19103
Phone: 215-814-3147
Fax: 215-814-30001
E-mail: carr.cornelius@epamail.epa.gov

Gary Carroll
Office of Environmental Justice
Office of Enforcement and Compliance
Assurance
U.S. Environmental Protection Agency
1200 Pennsylvania Avenue, NW, (MC 2201A)
Washington, DC 20460
Phone: 202-564-2404
Fax: 202-501-0740
E-mail: Not Provided

Daisy Carter
Director
Project Awake
Rt 2, Box 282
Coatopa, AL 35470
Phone: 205-652-6823
Fax: 205-652-4320
E-mail: Not Provided

Ellen Case
Office of the Administrator
U.S. Environmental Protection Agency
1200 Pennsylvania Avenue, NW, (MC 1102)
Washington, DC 20460
Phone: 202-260-4712
Fax: 202-260-3412
E-mail: Not Provided

Larry Charles
ONE/CHANE, Inc.
2065 Main Street
Hartford, CT 06120
Phone: 860-525-0190
Fax: 860-522-8266
E-mail: larry.charles@snet.net

Jerry Clifford
Deputy Regional Administrator
Region 6
U.S. Environmental Protection Agency
1445 Ross Avenue, Suite 1200
Dallas, TX 75202-2733
Phone: 214-665-2100
Fax: 214-665-6648
E-mail: clifford.jerry@epa.gov

Luke Cole
General Counsel
Center on Race, Poverty and the Environment
California Rural Legal Assistance Foundation
631 Howard Street, Suite 330
San Francisco, CA 94105-3907
Phone: 415-495-8990
Fax: 415-495-8849
E-mail: crpe@igc.apc.org

Samuel J. Coleman
Director
Compliance Assurance and Enforcement
Division (6EN)
Region 6
U.S. Environmental Protection Agency
1445 Ross Avenue, Suite 1200
Dallas, TX 75202-2733
Phone: 214-665-2210
Fax: 214-665-7446
E-mail: coleman.sam@epa.gov

Monica Abreu Conley
Department of Environmental Conservation
State of New York
50 Wolf Road (Room 627)
Albany, NY 12233-5500
Phone: 518-457-0090
Fax: 518-485-8478
E-mail: mlconley@gw.dec.state.ny.us

Gregg A. Cooke
Regional Administrator
Region 6
U.S. Environmental Protection Agency
1445 Ross Avenue, Suite 1200
Dallas, TX 75202-2733
Phone: 214-665-2100
Fax: 214-665-6648
E-mail: cooke.gregg@epa.gov

Tiffany Cooper
Office of Solid Waste and Emergency
Response
U.S. Environmental Protection Agency
1200 Pennsylvania Avenue, NW, (MC 5101)
Washington, DC 20460
Phone: 202-260-0859
Fax: 202-260-6606
E-mail: cooper.tiffany@epa.gov

Michael Corbin
Attorney
The Corbin Law Firm, P.C.
1718 M Street, NW, Suite 299
Washington, DC 20036
Phone: 703-897-1577
Fax: 703-897-9767
E-mail: mccorbin@cpcug.org

Leslie Cormier
Public Affairs Director
DuPont Specialty Chemicals
Barley Mill Plaza, Building 23, Room 1359
Routes 48 & 141
Wilmington, DE 19805
Phone: 302-992-4273
Fax: 302-892-1135
E-mail: leslie.a.cormier@usa.dupont.com

Elizabeth A. Cotsworth
Office of Solid Waste
Office of Solid Waste and Emergency
Response
U.S. Environmental Protection Agency
1200 Pennsylvania Avenue, NW, (MC 5301W)
Washington, DC 20460
Phone: 703-308-8895
Fax: 703-308-0513
E-mail: cotsworth.elizabeth@epa.gov

Ann Coyle
Office of Regional Counsel
Region 5
U.S. Environmental Protection Agency
77 West Jackson Boulevard, (C-14J)
Chicago, IL 60604
Phone: 312-886-2248
Fax: 312-886-0747
E-mail: coyle.ann@epa.gov

Martin Coyne
Associate Editor
Water Policy Report
Inside Washington Publishers
1225 Jefferson Davis Highway, Suite 1400
Arlington, VA 22202
Phone: 703-416-8564
Fax: 703-416-8543
E-mail: Not Provided

Jenny Craig
Office of Air and Radiation
U.S. Environmental Protection Agency
1200 Pennsylvania Avenue, NW, (MC 6103A)
Washington, DC 20460
Phone: 202-564-1674
Fax: 202-564-1557
E-mail: craig.jeneva@epa.gov

Elizabeth Crowe
Chemical Weapons Working Group
P.O. Box 467
Berea, KY 40403
Phone: 606-986-0868
Fax: 606-986-2695
E-mail: kefcrowe@acs.eku.edu

Fernando Cuevas
Vice President
Farm Labor Organizing Committee
326 East Maple Street
Winter Garden, FL 34787
Phone: 407-877-2949
Fax: 407-877-0031
E-mail: Not Provided

Erin Curran
Employees for Environmental Responsibility
Address Not Provided
Phone: 202-265-7337
Fax: Not Provided
E-mail: Not Provided

Vernell Cutter
CFEJ
1115 Habersham Street
Savannah, GA 31401
Phone: 912-236-6479
Fax: 912-236-7757
E-mail: v_cutter@yahoo.com

Clydia J. Cuykendall
Associate General Counsel
JC Penney
P.O. Box 1001
Dallas, TX 75301-1104
Phone: 972-431-1290
Fax: 972-431-1133
E-mail: cjcuyken@jcpenney.com

Lottie Dalton
N.B.R.E. Member
N.B.R.E.
P.O. Box 781
Baker, LA 70704
Phone: 225-775-3794
Fax: Not Provided
E-mail: Not Provided

Dagmar M. Darjean
Mossville Environmental Action Now
(M.E.A.N.), Inc.
4117 Perkins Avenue
Sulphur-Mossville, LA 70663
Phone: 337-882-7476
Fax: 337-882-7476
E-mail: delilith@aol.com

Lawrence Dark
5236 North East Cleveland
Portland, OR 97211
Phone: 503-318-5432
Fax: 503-727-1117
E-mail: ldark@orednet.org

Rebecca Davidson
Delaware Tribe of Western Oklahoma
P.O. Box 825
Anadarko, OK 73009
Phone: 405-247-2448
Fax: Not Provided
E-mail: aapanahkih@tanet.net

Katherine Dawes
Office of Policy and Reinvention
Office of Policy
U.S. Environmental Protection Agency
1200 Pennsylvania Avenue, NW, (MC 1802)
Washington, DC 20460
Phone: 202-260-8394
Fax: 202-260-3125
E-mail: dawes.katherine@epa.gov

Joanne Dea
Standards and Applied Science Division
Office of Water
U.S. Environmental Protection Agency
1200 Pennsylvania Avenue, NW, (MC 4305)
Washington, DC 20460
Phone: 202-260-0180
Fax: 202-260-4580
E-mail: dea.joanne@epa.gov

Carol Dennis
Office of Management and Budget
725 17th Street, NW, Room 8026
New Executive Office Building
Washington, DC 20503
Phone: 202-395-4822
Fax: 202-395-5836
E-mail: carol_r._dennis@omb.eop.gov

Michael J. DiBartolomeis
California Office of Environmental Health
Hazard Assessment
1515 Clay Street, 16th Floor
Oakland, CA 94612
Phone: 510-622-3164
Fax: 510-622-3218
E-mail: mdibarto@oehha.ca.gov

Trevor Smith Diggins
Vice President
Frontline Corporate Communications Inc.
22 Frederick Street, Suite 910
Kitchener, Ontario N2H 6M6
Phone: 888-848-9898
Fax: 519-741-9323
E-mail: diggins@onthefrontlines.com

Debra Dobson
Four Mile Hibernian Community Association
Inc.
2025 Four Mile lane
Charleston, SC 29405
Phone: 843-853-4548
Fax: 843-792-3757
E-mail: Not Provided

Richard T. Drury
Legal Director
Communities for a Better Environment
500 Howard Street, Suite 506
San Francisco, CA 94105
Phone: 415-243-8373
Fax: 415-243-8930
E-mail: richarddrury@hotmail.com

Delbert DuBois
Four Mile Hibernian Community Association, Inc.
2025 Four Mile Lane
Charleston, SC 29405
Phone: 843-853-4548
Fax: 843-792-3757
E-mail: Not Provided

Josephine DuBois
Four Mile Hibernian Community Association Inc.
2025 Four Mile lane
Charleston, SC 29405
Phone: 843-853-4548
Fax: 843-792-3757
E-mail: Not Provided

Frances Dubrowski
Attorney At Law
Law Offices of Frances Dubrowski
1320 19th Street, NW, Suite 200
Washington, DC 20036
Phone: 202-667-5795
Fax: 202-667-2302
E-mail: dubrowski@aol.com

Veronica Eady
Executive Office of Environmental Affairs
State of Massachusetts
100 Cambridge Street, 20th Floor
Boston, MA 02202
Phone: 617-626-1053
Fax: 617-626-1180
E-mail: veronica.eady@state.ma.us

T. Eaport
EDU
1010 Massachusettes Avenue, NW
Washngton, DC 20001
Phone: 202-289-4435
Fax: Not Provided
E-mail: Not Provided

Carl Edlund
Superfund Branch (6SF-L/N)
Region 6
U.S. Environmental Protection Agency
1445 Ross Avenue, Suite 1200
Dallas, TX 75202-2733
Phone: 214-665-2200
Fax: 214-665-6660
E-mail: edlund.carl@epa.gov

Chebryll C. Edwards
Office of Air and Radiation
U.S. Environmental Protection Agency
MD-15
Research Triangle Park, NC 27711
Phone: 919-541-5428
Fax: 919-541-0237
E-mail: edwards.chebryll@epa.gov

Jim Eichner
Environment & Natural Resources Division
U.S. Department of Justice
601 D Street, NW, Room 8036
Washington, DC 20004
Phone: 202-514-0624
Fax: 202-514-4231
E-mail: james.eichner@usdot.gov

Natalie Ellington
Water Management Division
Region 4
U.S. Environmental Protection Agency
61 Forsyth Street, SW
Atlanta, GA 30303
Phone: 404-562-9453
Fax: 404-562-9439
E-mail: ellington.natalie@epa.gov

Samantha Phillips Fairchild
Director
Office of Enforcement Compliance and Environmental Justice
Region 3
U.S. Environmental Protection Agency
1650 Arch Street
Philadelphia, PA 19103
Phone: 215-814-2106
Fax: 215-814-2905
E-mail: fairchild.samantha@epamail.epa.gov

Caron Falcouer
Region 4
U.S. Environmental Protection Agency
61 Forsythe Street
Atlanta, GA 30303
Phone: 404-562-8451
Fax: Not Provided
E-mail: Not Provided

Henry Falk
Assistant Administrator
Agency for Toxic Substances and Disease Registry
1600 Clifton Road, NE
Atlanta, GA 30333
Phone: 404-639-0700
Fax: 404-639-0744
E-mail: hxf1@cdc.gov

Joan Harrigan Farrelly
U.S. Environmental Protection Agency
1200 Pennsylvania Avenue, NW, (MC 4606)
Washington, DC 20460
Phone: 202-260-6672
Fax: 202-260-0732
E-mail: farrelly.joan@epa.gov

Denise Feiber
Environmental Science & Engineering, Inc.
404 SW 140th Terrace
Newberry, FL 32669-3000
Phone: 352-333-2605
Fax: 352-333-6633
E-mail: ddfeiber@esemail.com

Nigel Fields
Office of Research and Development
U.S. Environmental Protection Agency
1200 Pennsylvania Avenue, NW, (MC 8723E)
Washington, DC 20460
Phone: 202-564-6936
Fax: 202-565-2448
E-mail: fields.negel@epa.gov

Timothy Fields, Jr.
Assistant Administrator
Office of Solid Waste and Emergency Response
U.S. Environmental Protection Agency
1200 Pennsylvania Avenue, NW, (MC 5101)
Washington, DC 20460
Phone: 202-260-4610
Fax: 202-260-3527
E-mail: fields.timothy@epa.gov

LaTonya Flint
Public Affairs Specialist
Region 7
U.S. Environmental Protection Agency
901 North 5th Street
Kansas City, KS 66101
Phone: 913-551-7555
Fax: 913-551-7066
E-mail: flint.latonya@epa.gov

Terry Flynn
Frontline Corporate Communications
Incorporated
22 Federick Street, Suite 910
Kitchener, Ontario N2H 6M6
Phone: 519-741-9011
Fax: 519-741-9323
E-mail: flynn@onthefrontlines.com

Paula Forbis
Environmental Health Coalition
1717 Kettner Boulevard, Suite 100
San Diego, CA 92101
Phone: 619-235-0281
Fax: 619-232-3670
E-mail: Not Provided

Catherine Fox
Environmental Accountability Division
Region 4
U.S. Environmental Protection Agency
61 Forsyth Street, SW
Atlanta, GA 30303
Phone: 404-562-9634
Fax: 404-562-9598
E-mail: fox.catherine@epa.gov

Rosa Franklin
Washington State Senator
409 Legislative Building
P.O. Box 40482
Olympia, WA 98504-0482
Phone: 360-786-7656
Fax: 360-786-7524
E-mail: franklin_ro@leg.wa.gov

Anna Frazier
Coordinator
DINE CArE
HC-63, Box 263
Winslow, AZ 86047
Phone: 602-657-3291
Fax: 602-657-3319
E-mail: dinecare@cnetco.com

Myra Frazier
Office of Policy
U.S. Environmental Protection Agency
1200 Pennsylvania Avenue, NW, (MC 2175)
Washington, DC 20460
Phone: 202-260-2784
Fax: 202-260-6405
E-mail: frazier.myra@epamail.epa.gov

Katharine Fredriksen
Public Affairs
Koch Industries, Inc.
1450 G Street, NW, Suite 445
Washington, DC 20005
Phone: 202-737-1977
Fax: 202-737-8111
E-mail: fredrikk@kochind.com

Jennifer Friday
Joint Center for Political and Economic Studies
1090 Vermont Avenue, NW, Suite 1100
Washington, DC 20005
Phone: 202-789-3500
Fax: 202-789-6390
E-mail: jfriday@jointcenter.org

Gregory Fried
Manufacturing Energy and Transportation
Division
Office of Environment and Compliance
Assurance
U.S. Environmental Protection Agency
1200 Pennsylvania Avenue, NW, (MC 2223A)
Washington, DC 20460
Phone: 202-564-7016
Fax: 202-564-0050
E-mail: fried.gregory@epa.gov

James Friloux
Ombudsman
Louisiana Department of Environmental Quality
P.O. Box 82263
Baton Rouge, LA 70884
Phone: 225-765-0735
Fax: 225-765-0746
E-mail: jim_f@deq.state.la.us

Jan Fritz
University of Cincinnati
7300 Aracoma Forest Drive
Cincinnati, OH 45237
Phone: 513-556-0208
Fax: 513-556-1274
E-mail: jan.fritz@uc.edu

Arnita Gadson
University of Louisville, KY
West Co Environmental Task Force
1015 West Chestnut
Louisville, KY 40203
Phone: 502-852-4609
Fax: 502-852-4610
E-mail: ahgads01@gwise.lou.edu or
ahgads01@belknap.pob

Arnoldo Garcia
Regional Community Organizer
Urban Habitat Program
P.O. Box 29908 Presidio Station
San Francisco, CA 94129
Phone: 415-561-3332
Fax: 415-561-3334
E-mail: agarcia@igc.apc.org

Linda Garczynski
Director
Outreach and Special Projects Staff
Office of Solid Waste and Emergency
Response
U.S. Environmental Protection Agency
1200 Pennsylvania Avenue, NW, (MC 5101)
Washington, DC 20460
Phone: 202-260-1223
Fax: 202-260-6606
E-mail: garczynski.linda@epa.gov

Eileen Gauna
Professor
Southwestern University Law School
675 South Westmoreland Avenue
Los Angeles, CA 90005
Phone: 213-738-6752-
Fax: 213-383-1688
E-mail: egauna@swlaw.edu

Clarice Gaylord
Special Assistant to the Regional Administrator
San Diego Border Liaison Office
Region 9
U.S. Environmental Protection Agency
610 West Ash Street, Suite 703
San Diego, CA 92101
Phone: 619-235-4767
Fax: 619-235-4771
E-mail: gaylord.clarice@epa.gov

Michel Gelobter
Graduate Department of Public Administration
Rutgers University
714 Hill Hall
Newark, NJ 07102
Phone: 209-353-5093 ext. 18
Fax: 209-927-4574
E-mail: gelobter@andromeda.rutgers.edu

Michael Gerrard
Arnold & Porter
399 Park Avenue, 35th Floor
New York, NY 10022
Phone: 212-715-1000
Fax: 212-715-1399
E-mail: michael_gerrard@aporter.com

Gail C. Ginsberg
Office of Regional Counsel
Region 5
U.S. Environmental Protection Agency
77 West Jackson Boulevard
Chicago, IL 60640
Phone: 312-886-6675
Fax: 312-886-0747
E-mail: ginsberg.gail@epa.gov

Myles Glasgow
Attorney
4465 Greenwich Road, NW
Washington, DC 20007
Phone: 202-625-6233
Fax: 202-625-6914
E-mail: nvleopard@aol.com

Daniel Gogal
Office of Environmental Justice
Office of Enforcement and Compliance
Assurance
U.S. Environmental Protection Agency
1200 Pennsylvania Avenue, NW, (MC 2201A)
Washington, DC 20460
Phone: 202-564-2576
Fax: 202-501-0740
E-mail: gogal.danny@epa.gov

Renee Goins
Environmental Protection Specialist
Office of Environmental Justice
Office of Enforcement and Compliance
Assurance
U.S. Environmental Protection Agency
1200 Pennsylvania Avenue, NW, (MC 2201A)
Washington, DC 20460
Phone: 202-564-2598
Fax: 202-501-0740
E-mail: goins.renee@epa.gov

Rhonda Golder
E.J. Coordinator
Office of Enforcement and Compliance
Assurance
U.S. Environmental Protection Agency
1200 Pennsylvania Avenue, NW, (MC 2222A)
Washington, DC 20004
Phone: 202-564-5088
Fax: 202-501-0411
E-mail: rhonda.golder@epamail.epa.gov

Ann Goode
Director
Office of Civil Rights
U.S. Environmental Protection Agency
1200 Pennsylvania Avenue, NW, (MC 1201)
Washington, DC 20460
Phone: Not Provided
Fax: Not Provided
E-mail: goode.ann@epa.gov

Wendy Graham
Office of International Activities
U.S. Environmental Protection Agency
1200 Pennsylvania Avenue, NW, (MC 2610R)
Washington, DC 20460
Phone: 202-564-6602
Fax: 202-565-2407
E-mail: graham.wendy@epa.gov

Lorraine L. Granado
Cross Community Coalition
2332 East 46th Avenue
Denver, CO 80216
Phone: 303-292-3203
Fax: 303-292-3341
E-mail: lorrgranado@yahoo.com

Running Grass
Environmental Specialist
Region 9
U.S. Environmental Protection Agency
75 Hawthorne Street
San Francisco, CA 94105
Phone: 415-744-1205
Fax: Not Provided
E-mail: Not Provided

Richard Green
Director
Waste Management Division
Region 4
U.S. Environmental Protection Agency
61 Forsyth Street, SW
Atlanta, GA 30303
Phone: 404-562-8651
Fax: 404-562-8063
E-mail: green.richard@epa.gov

Daniel Greenbaum
Health Effects Institute
955 Massachusetts Avenue
Cambridge, MA 02139
Phone: 617-876-6700
Fax: 617-876-6709
E-mail: dgreenbaum@healtheffects.org

Jamie Grodsky
Senior Advisor to the General Counsel
Office of Environmental Justice
Office of Enforcement and Compliance
Assurance
U.S. Environmental Protection Agency
1200 Pennsylvania Avenue, NW, (MC 2201A)
Washington, DC 20460
Phone: 202-260-8039 ext. '
Fax: 202-260-8046
E-mail: Not Provided

Richard Grow
Region 9
U.S. Environmental Protection Agency
75 Hawthorne Street
San Francisco, CA 94105
Phone: 415-744-1203
Fax: 415-744-1076
E-mail: grow.richard@epamail.epa.gov

J. Grumet
NESCAUM
129 Portland Street
Boston, MA 02114
Phone: 617-367-8540
Fax: 617-742-9162
E-mail: jgrumet@nescaum.org

Tony Guadagno
Assistant General Counsel
Office of General Counsel
U.S. Environmental Protection Agency
1200 Pennsylvania Avenue, NW, (MC 2322)
Washington, DC 20460
Phone: 202-564-5537
Fax: 202-564-5541
E-mail: guadagno.tony@epa.gov

James Habron, Jr.
Penn State University
736 Maple Road
Pleasantville, NJ 08232
Phone: 609-645-1921
Fax: Not Provided
E-mail: jwh17@earthlink.net

George Hagevik
National Conference of State Legislatures
1560 Broadway, Suite 700
Denver, CO 80202
Phone: 303-830-2200
Fax: 303-863-8003
E-mail: george.hagevik@ncsl.org

Beth Hailstock
Director
Environmental Justice Center
Cincinnati Health Department
3101 Burnet Avenue
Cincinnati, OH 45229
Phone: 513-357-7206
Fax: 513-357-7262
E-mail: beth.hailstock@chdburn.rcc.org

Loren Hall
Office of Civil Rights
U.S. Environmental Protection Agency
1200 Pennsylvania Avenue, NW, (MC 1201)
Washington, DC 20460
Phone: 202-260-3931
Fax: 202-260-4580
E-mail: hall.loren@epamail.epa.gov

Robert W. Hall
Office of Solid Waste
Office of Solid Waste and Emergency
Response
U.S. Environmental Protection Agency
1200 Pennsylvania Avenue, NW
Washington, DC 20024
Phone: 703-308-8432
Fax: Not Provided
E-mail: hall.robert@epa.gov

Martin Halper
Senior Science Advisor
Office of Environmental Justice
Office of Enforcement and Compliance
Assurance
U.S. Environmental Protection Agency
1200 Pennsylvania Avenue, NW, (MC 2201A)
Washington, DC 20460
Phone: 202-564-2601
Fax: 202-501-0740
E-mail: halper.martin@epa.gov

Brad Hamilton
Director
Native American Affairs Office
Dept. Of Human Resources
State of Kansas
1430 S.W. Topeka Boulevard
Topeka, KS 66612-1853
Phone: 785-368-7319
Fax: 785-296-1795
E-mail: bbhamilt@hr.state.ks.us

Denise Hamilton
Environmental Engineer-NPDES Permitting
Region 6
U.S. Environmental Protection Agency
1446 Ross Avenue
Dallas, TX
Phone: 214-665-2775
Fax: 214-665-2191
E-mail: hamilton.denise@epa.gov

James Hamilton
Associate Professor
Duke University
Box 90245 Duke
Durham, NC 27708
Phone: 919-613-7358
Fax: 919-681-8288
E-mail: jayth@pps.duke.edu

Tony Hanson
American Indian Environmental Office
U.S. Environmental Protection Agency
1200 Pennsylvania Avenue, NW, (MC 4104)
Washington, DC 20460
Phone: 202-260-8106
Fax: 202-260-7509
E-mail: Not Provided

William Harnett
Acting Director
Information Transfer and Program Integration
Division
Office of Air and Radiation
U.S. Environmental Protection Agency
MD-12
Research Triangle Park, NC 27711
Phone: 919-541-4979
Fax: 919-541-4979
E-mail: harnett.bill@epa.gov

Alisa Harris
Office of Chief Counsel
State of Pennsylvania
Rachel Carson Office Building, P.O. Box 2063
Harrisburg, PA 17105-2063
Phone: 717-783-9731
Fax: 717-783-8926
E-mail: Not Provided

Reginald Harris
Environmental Justice Coordinator
Region 3
U.S. Environmental Protection Agency
1650 Arch Street, (3EC00)
Philadelphia, PA 19103
Phone: 215-814-2988
Fax: 215-814-2905
E-mail: harris.reggie@epa.gov

Rita Harris
Community Living in Peace, Inc.
1373 South Avenue
Memphis, TN 38106
Phone: 901-948-6002
Fax: 901-948-6002
E-mail: xundu@usa.net

Stuart Harris
Department of Natural Resources
Confederated Tribes of the Umatilla
P.O. Box 638
Pendelton, OR 97801
Phone: 541-276-0105
Fax: 541-278-5380
E-mail: Not Provided

Rose Harvell
Environmental Justice Coordinator
Office of Site Remediation Enforcement
Office of Enforcement and Compliance
Assurance
U.S. Environmental Protection Agency
1200 Pennsylvania Avenue, NW, (MC 2273A)
Washington, DC 20460
Phone: 202-564-6056
Fax: 202-564-0074
E-mail: harvell.rose@epa.gov

Albertha D. Hasten
Concerned Citizens of Iberville Parish
32365 Doc Dean Street
White Castle, LA 70788
Phone: 225-545-1034
Fax: 225-545-1034
E-mail: Not Provided

Melva J. Hayden
Environmental Justice Coordinator
Office of the Regional Administrator
Region 2
U.S. Environmental Protection Agency
290 Broadway, Room 2637
New York City, NY 10007
Phone: 212-637-5027
Fax: 212-637-4943
E-mail: hayden.melva@epa.gov

Peter Hayes
Associate Editor
Superfund Report
Inside Washington Publishers
1225 Jefferson Davis Highway, Suite 1400
Arlington, VA 22202
Phone: 703-416-8518
Fax: 703-416-8543
E-mail: superfundreport@yahoo.com

Stephen Heare
Acting Director
Permits and State Programs Division
Office of Solid Waste and Emergency
Response
U.S. Environmental Protection Agency
1200 Pennsylvania Avenue, NW, (MC 5303 W)
Washington, DC 20460
Phone: 703-308-8801
Fax: 703-308-8617
E-mail: heare.stephen@epamail.epa.gov

Alan Hecht
Principal Deputy Assistant Administrator
Office of International Activities
U.S. Environmental Protection Agency
1200 Pennsylvania Avenue, NW
Washington, DC 20450
Phone: 202-564-6600
Fax: Not Provided
E-mail: Not Provided

Judy Hecht
Office of Water
U.S. Environmental Protection Agency
1200 Pennsylvania Avenue, NW, (MC 4102)
Washington, DC 20460
Phone: 202-260-5682
Fax: 202-401-3372
E-mail: hecht.judy@epa.gov

Jody Henneke
Director - Office of public Asistance
Texas Natural Resource Conservation
Commission
P.O. Box 13087 (MC 108)
Austin, TX 73087
Phone: 512-239-4085
Fax: 512-239-4007
E-mail: jhenneke@tnrcc.state.tx.us.com

Steven Herman
Assistant Administrator
Office of Enforcement and Compliance
Assurance
U.S. Environmental Protection Agency
1200 Pennsylvania Avenue, NW, (MC 2201A)
Washington, DC 20460
Phone: 202-564-2440
Fax: 202-501-3842
E-mail: herman.steven@epa.gov

Ivie Higgins
Coalition for Environmentally Responsible
Economies
11 Arlington Street, 6th Floor
Boston, MA 02116
Phone: 617-247-0700
Fax: 617-267-5400
E-mail: higgins@ceres.org

Barry Hill
Director
Office of Environmental Justice
Office of Enforcement and Compliance
Assurance
U.S. Environmental Protection Agency
1200 Pennsylvania Avenue, NW, (MC 2201A)
Washington, DC 22460
Phone: 202-564-2515
Fax: 202-501-0964
E-mail: hill.barry@epa.gov

Kathleen Hill
Native American Studies Department
Humbolt State University
Arcata, CA 95521
Phone: 707-826-4322
Fax: 707-826-4418
E-mail: ksh7@axe.humboldt.edu

Pat K. Hill
Senior Manager
Federal Regulatory Affairs
Georgia-Pacific Corporation
1875 Eye Street, NW, Suite 775
Washington, DC 20006
Phone: 202-659-3600
Fax: 202-223-1398
E-mail: phill@gapac.com

Jennifer Hill-Kelley
Oneida Nation of Wisconsin
P.O. Box 365
3759 West Mason Street
Oneida, WI 54155
Phone: 920-497-5812
Fax: 920-496-7883
E-mail: jhillkel@oneidanation.org

Kendolyn Hodges-Simons
Attorney Advisor
Office of Enforcement and Regulatory
Compliance
Environmental Health Administration
D.C. Department of Health
51 N Street, NE, 6th Floor
Washington, DC 20002
Phone: 202-535-2609
Fax: 202-535-1359
E-mail: Not Provided

Pierre Hollingsworth
NAACP
526 Pacific Avenue (TH-4)
Atlantic City, NJ 08401
Phone: 609-345-5298
Fax: 609-345-5230
E-mail: Not Provided

Mike Holloway
Program Analyst
Indoor Environments Division
Office of Air and Radiation
U.S. Environmental Protection Agency
1200 Pennsylvania Avenue, NW, (MC 6609J)
Washington, DC 20460
Phone: 202-564-9426
Fax: 202-565-2039
E-mail: holloway.mike@epa.gov

Michael K. Holmes
Northside Education Center
St. Louis Community College
4666 Natural Bridge
St. Louis, MO 63115
Phone: 314-381-3822
Fax: 314-381-4637
E-mail: mholmes@ccm.stlcc.cc.mo.us

Robert Holmes
Director
Southern Center for Studies in Public Policy
Clark Atlanta University
223 James P. Brawley Drive, SW
Atlanta, GA 30314
Phone: 404-880-8089
Fax: 404-880-8090
E-mail: bholmes@cau.edu

Brian Holtzclaw
Environmental Justice Waste Management
Division
Region 4
U.S. Environmental Protection Agency
61 Forsyth Street, SW
Atlanta, GA 30303
Phone: 404-562-8684
Fax: 404-562-8628
E-mail: holtzclaw.brian@epa.gov

Savonala "Savi" Horne
Staff Attorney
Land Loss Prevention Project
P.O. Box 179
Durham, NC 27713
Phone: 919-682-5969
Fax: 919-688-5596
E-mail: savillpp@mindspring.com

Nancy Howard
Water Resources Planner
Newport News Waterworks
2600 Washington Avenue
Newport News, VA 23607
Phone: 757-926-7177
Fax: 757-926-7179
E-mail: nhowardoci.newport-news.va.us

Matthew Huntes
The EOP Group, Inc.
819 7th Street, NW
Washington, DC 20001
Phone: 202-833-8940
Fax: 202-833-8945
E-mail: mfhuntes@819eagle.com

Daniel Isales
Office of Environmental Justice
Region 3
U.S. Environmental Protection Agency
1650 Arch Street
Philadelphia, PA 19103-2029
Phone: 215-814-2647
Fax: 215-814-2905
E-mail: isales.daniel@epamail.epa.gov

Ken Israels
Region 9
U.S. Environmental Protection Agency
75 Hawthorne Street
San Francisco, CA 94105
Phone: 415-744-1194
Fax: 415-744-1076
E-mail: israels.ken@epamail.epa.gov

Rose Jackson
Community Relations Specialist
Waste Management Division
Region 4
U.S. Environmental Protection Agency
61 Forsyth Street, SW
Atlanta, GA 30303
Phone: 404-562-8940
Fax: 404-562-8896
E-mail: jackson.rose@epamail.epa.gov

Sarah James
Tribal Member
Council of Aphabascan Tribal Governments
P.O. Box 51
Artic Village, AK 99722
Phone: 907-587-5315
Fax: 907-587-5900
E-mail: not provided

Annabelle E. Jaramillo
Citizens' Representative
Office of the Governor
State of Oregon
160 State Capitol
Salem, OR 97310
Phone: 503-378-5116
Fax: 503-378-6827
E-mail: annabelle.e.jaramillo@state.or.us

Karla Johnson
Environmental Justice Regional Team
Manager
Region 5
U.S. Environmental Protection Agency
77 West Jackson Boulevard (T-16J)
Chicago, IL 60604
Phone: 312-886-5993
Fax: 312-886-2737
E-mail: johnson.karla@epa.gov

Michael Johnson
Real Estate Investor
NAACP
1619 Columbia Avenue
Atlantic City, NJ 08401
Phone: 609-345-5298
Fax: Not Provided
E-mail: Not Provided

Sabrina Johnson
Policy Analyst
Office of Air and Radiation
U.S. Environmental Protection Agency
1200 Pennsylvania Avenue, NW
Washington, DC 20460
Phone: 202-564-1173
Fax: 202-564-1554
E-mail: johnson.sabrina@epa.gov

Khanna Johnston
Region 6
U.S. Environmental Protection Agency
1445 Ross Avenue, (6RA-DJ)
Dallas, TX 75202
Phone: 214-665-2716
Fax: 214-665-6490
E-mail: johnston.khanna@epamail.epa.gov

Carolyn Jones-Gray
Frederick Douglas Community Improvement
Council
2009 18th Street, SE
Washington, DC 20020
Phone: 202-678-3532
Fax: Not Provided
E-mail: Not Provided

Teresa Juarez
New Mexico Alliance
P.O. Box 759
Chimago, NM 87522
Phone: 505-351-2404
Fax: 505-351-1031
E-mail: tjuarez@la-tierra.com

Rochele Kadish
Office of the Administrator
U.S. Environmental Protection Agency
1200 Pennsylvania Avenue, NW, (MC 1108A)
Washington, DC 20460
Phone: 202-564-3106
Fax: 202-501-0062
E-mail: kadish.rochele@epa.gov

Ntale Kajumba
Environmental Justice Team
Region 4
U.S. Environmental Protection Agency
61 Forsyth Street, SW
Atlanta, GA 30310
Phone: 404-562-9620
Fax: Not Provided
E-mail: kajumba.ntale@epamail.epa.gov

Bob Keccam
Office of Air and Radiation
U.S. Environmental Protection Agency
MD-12
Research Triangle Park, NC 27711
Phone: 919-541-4028
Fax: 919-541-4028
E-mail: kellam.bob@epa.gov

Jeff Keohane
Attorney Advisor
Office of General Counsel
U.S. Environmental Protection Agency
1200 Pennsylvania Avenue, NW, (MC 2322)
Washington, DC 20460
Phone: 202-564-5548
Fax: 202-260-5541
E-mail: keohane.geffrey@epa.gov

Derrick Kimbrough
Community Involvement Coordinator
Office of Public Affairs
Region 5
U.S. Environmental Protection Agency
77 West Jackson Boulevard (P-19J)
Chicago, IL 60604
Phone: 312-886-9749
Fax: 312-353-1155
E-mail: kimbrough.derrick@epa.gov

Daphne King
Office Automation Clerk
Region 7
U.S. Environmental Protection Agency
901 North 5th Street
Kansas City, KS 66101
Phone: 913-551-7815
Fax: 913-551-7941
E-mail: king.daphne@epa.gov

Karen King
Policy Analyst
MBD, Inc.
1100 Connecticut Avenue. N.W. Suite 300
Washington, DC 20036
Phone: 202-429-1800
Fax: 202-429-8655
E-mail: karking@worldnet.att.net

Marva E. King
Office of Environmental Justice
Office of Enforcement and Compliance
Assurance
U.S. Environmental Protection Agency
1200 Pennsylvania Avenue, NW, (MC 2201A)
Washington, DC 20460
Phone: 202-564-2599
Fax: 202-501-0740
E-mail: king.marva@epa.gov

Michelle W. King
Office of Environmental Justice
Office of Enforcement and Compliance
Assurance
U.S. Environmental Protection Agency
1200 Pennsylvania Avenue, NW, (MC 2201A)
Washington, DC 20460
Phone: 202-564-4287
Fax: 202-501-0740
E-mail: king.michelle-w@epa.gov

Toshia King
Office of Waste
Office of Solid Waste And Emergency
Response
U.S. Environmental Protection Agency
1200 Pennsylvania Avenue, NW, (MC 5303W)
Washington, DC 20746
Phone: 703-308-7033
Fax: 703-308-8617
E-mail: Not Provided

Pamela J. Kingfisher
Director
Shining Waters
Box 182
Rowe, NM 87562
Phone: 505-757-3382
Fax: 505-757-3382
E-mail: pamejean@roadrunner.com

Jackie Kittrell
General Counsel
Environmental Health Network
318 Lynnwood
Knoxville, TN 37918
Phone: 423-522-1139
Fax: 423-689-8297
E-mail: jackieo@mindspring.com

David Klauder
Director, Regional Staff
Office of Research and Development
U.S. Environmental Protection Agency
1200 Pennsylvania Avenue, NW
Washington, DC 20460
Phone: 202-564-6496
Fax: Not Provided
E-mail: Not Provided

Michele L. Knorr
Office of General Counsel
U.S. Environmental Protection Agency
1200 Pennsylvania Avenue, NW, (MC 2333A)
Washington, DC 20460
Phone: 202-564-5631
Fax: 202-564-5644
E-mail: knorr.michele@epa.gov

Robert Knox
Associate Director
Office of Environmental Justice
Office of Enforcement and Compliance
Assurance
U.S. Environmental Protection Agency
1200 Pennsylvania Avenue, NW, (MC 2201A)
Washington, DC 20460
Phone: 202-564-2604
Fax: 202-501-0740
E-mail: knox.robert@epa.gov

Myron O. Knudson
Director
Superfund Division
Region 6
U.S. Environmental Protection Agency
1445 Ross Avenue, Suite 1200
Dallas, TX 75202-2733
Phone: 214-665-6701
Fax: 214-665-7330
E-mail: knudson.myron@epa.gov

Cassandra Koutalidis
Alternative Resources, Inc.
9 Pond Lane
Concord, MA 01742
Phone: 978-371-2054
Fax: 978-371-7269
E-mail: ckoutalidis@alt-res.com

Andrea Kreiner
Delaware Department of Natural Resources &
Environmental Control
89 Kings Highway
Dover, DE 19901
Phone: 302-739-4403
Fax: 302-739-6242
E-mail: akreiner@state.de.us

Arnold Kuzmack
Office of Water
U.S. Environmental Protection Agency
1200 Pennsylvania Avenue, NW
Washington, DC 20460
Phone: 202-260-5821
Fax: 202-260-5394
E-mail: kuzmack.arnold@epa.gov

Wendy Laird-Benner
Region 9
U.S. Environmental Protection Agency
75 Hawthorne Street, WTR - 4
San Francisco, CA 94105-3901
Phone: 415-744-1168
Fax: 415-744-1078
E-mail: laird-benner.wendy@epamail.epa.gov

Brad A. Lambert
Harris, DeVille and Associates, Inc.
307 France Street
Baton Rouge, LA 70802
Phone: 225-344-0381
Fax: 225-336-0211
E-mail: blambert@hdaissues.com

Wesley Lambert
Region 4
U.S. Environmental Protection Agency
3446 Rock Creek Drive
Rex, GA 30273
Phone: 770-968-3270
Fax: 404-562-8835
E-mail: lambert.wesley@epa.gov

David LaRoche
Senior Advisor-Tribal Programs
Office of Air and Radiation
U.S. Environmental Protection Agency
1200 Pennsylvania Avenue, NW, (MC 6604J)
Washington, DC
Phone: 202-260-7652
Fax: 202-260-8509
E-mail: laroche.david@epamail.epa.gov

Gretchen Latowsky
Project Manager
JSI Center for Environmental Health Studies
44 Farnsworth Street
Boston, MA 02210
Phone: 617-482-9485
Fax: 617-482-0617
E-mail: glatowsky@jsi.com

Richard Lazarus
Professor
Georgetown University Law Center
600 New Jersey Avenue, NW
Washington, DC 20001
Phone: 202-662-9129
Fax: 202-662-9408
E-mail: lazarusr@law.georgetown.edu

Adora Iris Lee
Minister for Environmental Justice
United Church of Christ
5113 Georgia Avenue, NW
Washington, DC 20011
Phone: 202-291-1593
Fax: 202-291-3933
E-mail: adoracrj@aol.com

Charles Lee
Associate Director
Office of Environmental Justice
Office of Enforcement and Compliance
Assurance
U.S. Environmental Protection Agency
1200 Pennsylvania Avenue, NW, (MC 2201A)
Washington, DC 20460
Phone: 202-564-2597
Fax: 202-501-0740
E-mail: lee.charles@epa.gov

Carol Leftwich
Project Manager
Environmental Council of the States
444 North Capitol Street, NW, Suite 305
Washington, DC 20001
Phone: 202-624-3660
Fax: 202-624-3666
E-mail: leftwich@sso.org

Jacqueline Lescott
Regulatory Representative
Associated Builders & Contractors
1300 N. 17th Street, Suite 800
Rosslyn, VA 22209
Phone: 703-812-2036
Fax: 703-812-8202
E-mail: lescott@abc.org

Michael Letourneau
Region 10
U.S. Environmental Protection Agency
1200 Sixth Avenue (CEJ-163)
Seattle, WA 98101
Phone: 206-553-1687
Fax: 206-553-7176
E-mail: letourneau.mike@epa.gov

Frederick Leutner
Chief, Water Quality Standards Branch
Office of Water
U.S. Environmental Protection Agency
1200 Pennsylvania Avenue, NW, (MC 4305)
Washington, DC 20460
Phone: 202-260-1542
Fax: 202-260-9830
E-mail: leutner.fred@epa.gov

Steven Levy
Office of Solid Waste
Office of Solid Waste and Emergency
Response
U.S. Environmental Protection Agency
1200 Pennsylvania Avenue, NW, (MC 5306 W)
Washington, DC 20460
Phone: 703-308-7267
Fax: 703-308-8686
E-mail: levy.steve@epa.gov

Sheila Lewis
Office of Environmental Justice
Office of Enforcement and Compliance
Assurance
U.S. Environmental Protection Agency
1200 Pennsylvania Avenue, NW, (MC 2201A)
Washington, DC 20460
Phone: 202-564-0163
Fax: 202-501-0740
E-mail: Not Provided

Sarah Lile
Director of Environmental Affairs
Department of Environmental Affairs
Region 5
U.S. Environmental Protection Agency
660 Woodward Avenue, Suite 1650
Detroit, MI 48226
Phone: 313-237-3092
Fax: 313-224-1547
E-mail: Not Provided

Benjamin Lim
Chemist
Office of Prevention, Pesticides, and Toxic
Substances
U.S. Environmental Protection Agency
1200 Pennsylvania Avenue, NW, (MC 7404)
Washington, DC 20460
Phone: 202-260-1509
Fax: 202-260-3453
E-mail: lim.benjamin@epa.gov

L. Diane Long
North Carolina Department of Environment
and Natural Resources
1601 Mail Service Center
Raleigh, NC 27699-2601
Phone: 919-715-4195
Fax: 919-715-3060
E-mail: diane.long@ncmail.net

Sylvia Lowrance
Deputy Administrator
Office of Enforcement and Compliance
Assurance
U.S. Environmental Protection Agency
1200 Pennsylvania Avenue, NW, (MC 2101A)
Washington, DC 20460
Phone: 202-260-7960
Fax: 202-501-3842
E-mail: lowrance.sylvia@epa.gov

Zack Lyde
Director
Save the People
P.O. Box 1994
Brunswick, GA 31521
Phone: 912-265-1275
Fax: 912-265-7008
E-mail: Not Provided

Pamela Lyons
Director
Office of Equal Opportunity, Contract
Assistance & Env. Equity
New Jersey Department of Environmental
Protection
P.O. Box 402
Trenton, NJ 08625
Phone: 609-984-9742
Fax: 609-984-9789
E-mail: plyons@dep.state.nj.us

Michael J. Lythcott
Citizens Against Toxic Exposure
6 Julian Way
Marlboro, NJ 07746-1615
Phone: 723-617-2076
Fax: 723-617-2071
E-mail: adeyemi@world.oberlin.edu

Jim MacDonald
Trustee
Pittsburg (California) Unified School District
274 Pebble Beach Loop
Pittsburg, CA 94565
Phone: 925-439-7665
Fax: 925-473-1886
E-mail: jmacdonald@pittsburg.k12.ca.us

Alfonse Mannato
Senior Regulatory Analyst
American Petrolem Institute
1220 L Street, NW
Washington, DC 20005-4070
Phone: 202-6828325
Fax: 202-682-8031
E-mail: mannatoa@api.org

Enrique Manzanilla
Region 9
U.S. Environmental Protection Agency
75 Hawthorne Street, CMD - 1
San Francisco, CA 94105
Phone: 415-744-1015
Fax: 415-744-1598
E-mail: manzanilla.enrique@epa.gov

Freya Margand
Environmental Protection Specialist
Office of Solid Waste/PSPD
Office of Solid Waste and Emergency
Response
U.S. Environmental Protection Agency
1200 Pennsylvania Avenue, NW, (MC 5303W)
Washington, DC 20460
Phone: 703-605-0633
Fax: 703-308-8638
E-mail: margand.freya@epa.gov

Jerry Martin
The DOW Chemical Company
2030 Dow Center
Midland, MI 48674
Phone: 517-636-8790
Fax: 517-636-0389
E-mail: jbmartin@dow.com

Lawrence Martin
Office of Research and Development
U.S. Environmental Protection Agency
1200 Pennsylvania Avenue, NW, (MC 8103R)
Washington, DC 20460
Phone: 202-564-6497
Fax: 202-564-2926
E-mail: martin.lawrence@epa.gov

Neftali Garcia Martinez
Scientific and Technical Services
RR-9 Buzon
1722, Cupey Alto
San Juan, 00926
Phone: 787-292-0620
Fax: 787-760-0496
E-mail: sctinc@caribe.net

Richard Mason
Shintech, Inc.
24 Greenway Plaza
Houston, TX 77046
Phone: 713-965-0713
Fax: 713-965-0629
E-mail: dmason@shin-tech.com

Alicia Maticardi
Office of Fair Housing and Equal Opportunity
U.S. Department of Housing and Urban
Development
451 7th Street, SW, Room 5249
Washington, DC 20410
Phone: 202-708-0614 ext. 7069
Fax: 202-708-1425
E-mail: alicia_maticardi@hud.gov

Paul Matthai
Pollution Prevention Division
Office of Prevention, Pesticides, and Toxic
Substances
U.S. Environmental Protection Agency
1200 Pennsylvania Avenue, NW, (MC 7409)
Washington, DC 20460
Phone: 202-260-3385
Fax: 202-260-0178
E-mail: matthai.paul@epamail.epa.gov

Doris Maxwell
Management Analyst
Office of Air Quality Planning and Standards
Office of Air and Radiation
U.S. Environmental Protection Agency
MD-13
Research Triangle Park, NC 27711
Phone: 919-541-5312
Fax: 919-541-0072
E-mail: maxwell.doris@epamail.epa.gov

Lisa Maybee
Environmental Director
1508 Route 438
Irving, NY 14081
Phone: 716-532-0024
Fax: 716-532-0035
E-mail: sniepd1@aol.com

Zulene Mayfield
Chair
Chester Residents Concerned for Quality
Living
2731 West Third Street
Chester, PA 19013
Phone: 610-485-6683
Fax: 610-485-5300
E-mail: crcqll@aol.com

John McCarroll
Region 9
U.S. Environmental Protection Agency
75 Hawthorne Street, WST-4
San Francisco, CA 94105
Phone: 415-744-2064
Fax: 415-744-1044
E-mail: mccarroll.john@epa.gov

Mildred McClain
Executive Director
Citizens for Environmental Justice
1115 Habersham Street
Savannah, GA 31401
Phone: 912-233-0907
Fax: 912-233-5105
E-mail: cfej@bellsouth.net

Keith McCoy
Director, Environmental Quality, Resources,
Environment & Regulation
National Association of Manufacturers
1331 Pennsylvania Avenue, NW
Washington, DC 20004-1790
Phone: 202-637-3175
Fax: 202-637-3182
E-mail: kmcoy@nam.org

Donna Gross McDaniel
Program Coordinator
Laborers-AGC Education and Training Fund
37 Deerfield Road
P.O. Box 37
Pomfret Center, CT 06259
Phone: 860-974-0800 ext. 109
Fax: 860-974-3157
E-mail: dmcdaniel@laborers-agc.org

Kate McGloon
Manager, External Relations
CMA
1300 Wilson Boulevard
Arlington, VA 22209
Phone: 703-741-5812
Fax: 703-741-6812
E-mail: kate_mcgloon@cmahq.com

Laura McKelvey
Environmental Scientist
Office of Air and Radiation
U.S. Environmental Protection Agency
MD-15
Research Triangle Park, NC 27711
Phone: 919-541-5497
Fax: 919-541-7690
E-mail: mckelvey.laura@epa.gov

Kara McKoy-Belle
Environmental Justice Office
Region 6
U.S. Environmental Protection Agency
1445 Ross Avenue, Suite 1200, (6EN)
Dallas, TX 75202-2733
Phone: 214-665-8337
Fax: 214-665-6660
E-mail: mckoy.kara.@epa.gov

Brian McLean
Acid Rain Division
Office of Air and Radiation
U.S. Environmental Protection Agency
1200 Pennsylvania Avenue, NW, (MC 6204J)

Phone: 202-564-9150
Fax: 202-565-2141
E-mail: mclean.brian@epa.gov

Tanya J. Meekins
Media Relations Office
Office of the Administrator
U.S. Environmental Protection Agency
1200 Pennsylvania Avenue, NW, (MC 1703)
Washington, DC 20460
Phone: 202-2601387
Fax: 202-260-3522
E-mail: meekins.tanya@epamail.gov

Jayne Michaud
Office of Solid Waste and Emergency
Response
U.S. Environmental Protection Agency
1200 Pennsylvania Avenue, NW, (MC 5204G)
Washington, DC 20460
Phone: 703-603-8847
Fax: 703-603-9104
E-mail: michaud.jayne@epa.gov

Vernice Miller-Travis
Partnership For Sustainable Brownfields
Redevelopment
104 Jewett Place
Bowie, MD 20721
Phone: Not Provided
Fax: 410-338-2751
E-mail: vmiller@nrdc.org

Dana Minerva
Deputy Assistant Administrator
Office of Water
U.S. Environmental Protection Agency
1200 Pennsylvania Avenue, NW, (MC 4101)
Washington, DC 20460
Phone: 202-260-5700
Fax: 202-260-5711
E-mail: minerva.dana@epa.gov

Marsha Minter
Special Assistant
Office of the Administrator
U.S. Environmental Protection Agency
1200 Pennsylvania Avenue, NW, (MC 1102)
Washington, DC 20460
Phone: 202-260-6626
Fax: 202-260-4852
E-mail: minter.marsha@epamail.gov

Cristina Miranda
Intern
Office of Environmental Justice
Office of Enforcement and Compliance
Assurance
U.S. Environmental Protection Agency
1200 Pennsylvania Avenue, NW, (MC 2201A)
Washington, DC 20460
Phone: 202-564-2636
Fax: 202-501-0740
E-mail: miranda.cristina@epa.gov

Harold Mitchell
Director
REGENISIS
101 Anita Drive
Spartanburg, SC 29302
Phone: 864-542-8420
Fax: 864-582-4062
E-mail: not provided

Rita M. Monroy
COSSMHO
1501 Sixteenth Street, NW
Washington, DC 20036
Phone: 202-797-4334
Fax: 202-797-4353
E-mail: rmonroy@cossmho.org

Lillian Mood, R.N.
Community Liaison
South Carolina Department of Health and
Environmental Control
2600 Bull Street
Columbia, SC 29201
Phone: 803-898-3929
Fax: 803-898-3931
E-mail: moodlh@columb30.dhec.state.sc.us

John R. Moody
Waste Management Division
Region 9
U.S. Environmental Protection Agency
75 Hawthorne Street, WST-4
San Francisco, CA 94105-3901
Phone: 415-744-2058
Fax: 415-538-5053
E-mail: moody.john@epamail.epa.gov

Alma Black Moore
Frontline Corporate Communications Inc.
2163 Airways Boulevard
Memphis, TN 38114
Phone: 901-544-0613
Fax: 901-544-0639
E-mail: ablack1@midsouth.rr.com

Anthony Moore
Director of Policy
Department of Environmental Quality
State of Virginia
629 E. Main Street
P.O. Box 10009
Richmond, VA 23240-0009
Phone: 804-698-4484
Fax: 804-698-4346
E-mail: aumoore@deq.state.va.us

Althea M. Moses
Program Manager
Office of Environmental Justice
Region 7
U.S. Environmental Protection Agency
726 Minnesota Avenue
Kansas City, KS 66101
Phone: 913-551-7649
Fax: 913-551-7976
E-mail: moses.althea@epa.gov

Edgar J. Mouton
Mossville Environmental Action Now
(M.E.A.N.), Inc.
3608 E. Burton
Sulphur, LA 70663
Phone: 337-625-8414
Fax: 337-882-7476
E-mail: meanmoss@yahoo.com

Kathryn Mutz
Natural Resources Law Center
University of Colorado School of Law
Campus Box 401
Boulder, CO 80309-0401
Phone: 303-492-1293
Fax: 303-492-1297
E-mail: kathryn.mutz@colorado.edu

Mildred Myers
South Carolina Envrionmental Watch
P.O. Box 373
Gadsden, SC 29052
Phone: 803-353-8423
Fax: 803-353-8427
E-mail: Not Provided

Oleda Myers
South CarolinaEnvironmental Water
P.O. Box 372
Gadsden, SC 29052
Phone: 803-353-8423
Fax: 803-353-8427
E-mail: omyers3@bellsouth.net

Vernon Myers
Permits
Office of Solid Waste and Emergency
Response
U.S. Environmental Protection Agency
1200 Pennsylvania Avenue, NW, (MC 5305W)
Washington, DC 20460
Phone: 703-308-8660
Fax: 703-308-8609
E-mail: myers.vernon@epamail.epa.gov

Paul Nadeau
Senior Process Manager for Reforms
Office of Emergency and Remedial Response
Office of Solid Waste and Emergency
Response
U.S. Environmental Protection Agency
1200 Pennsylvania Avenue, NW, (MC 5204G)
Washington, DC 20460
Phone: 703-603-8794
Fax: 703-603-9104
E-mail: nadeau.paul@epa.gov

Tia Newman-Fields
Office of Environmental Justice
Office of Enforcement and Compliance
Assurance
U.S. Environmental Protection Agency
1200 Pennsylvania Avenue, NW, (MC 2201A)
Washington, DC 20460
Phone: 202-564-2622
Fax: 202-505-0740
E-mail: newman-fields.tia@epamail.epa.gov

David Nicholas
Policy Analyst
Office of Solid Waste
Office of Solid Waste and Emergency
Response
U.S. Environmental Protection Agency
1200 Pennsylvania Avenue, NW, (MC 5103)
Washington, DC 20460
Phone: 202-260-4512
Fax: 202-401-1496
E-mail: nicholas.david@epa.gov

William Nitze
Assistant Administrator
Office of International Activities
U.S. Environmental Protection Agency
1200 Pennsylvania Avenue, NW, (MC 2670R)
Washington, DC 20460
Phone: Not Provided
Fax: Not Provided
E-mail: Not Provided

Kojo Nnamdi
Host, Public Interest
National Public Radio
Address Not Provided
Washington, DC 20460
Phone: Not Provided
Fax: Not Provided
E-mail: Not Provided

Duncan Norton
General Counsel
Texas National Resource Conservation
Commission
12100 N. Park 35 Circle
Austin, TX 78711
Phone: 523-239-5525
Fax: 512-239-5533
E-mail: Not Provided

Davy Obey
Associate Editor
Clean Air Report
1225 Jefferson Davis Highway, Suite 1400
Arlington, VA 22209
Phone: 703-416-8516
Fax: 703-416-8543
E-mail: sunrd@aol.com

Joyce Olin
Federal Facilities Enforcement Office
Office of Enforcement and Compliance
Assurance
U.S. Environmental Protection Agency
1200 Pennsylvania Avenue, NW, (MC 2261A)
Washington, DC 20460
Phone: 202-564-2582
Fax: 202-501-0644
E-mail: olin.joyce@epa.gov

Juan Orozco
Northwest Community Education Center
P.O. Box 800
Granger, WA 98932
Phone: 509-854-2222
Fax: 509-854-2223
E-mail: Not Provided

Richard B. Ossias
Air and Radiation Law Office
Office of Air and Radiation
U.S. Environmental Protection Agency
1200 Pennsylvania Avenue, NW, (MC 2344)
Washington, DC 20460
Phone: 202-260-7984
Fax: 202-260-0586
E-mail: ossias.richard@epa.gov

James Owens
Region 1
U.S. Environmental Protection Agency
One Congress Street, Suite 1100 (MIO)
Boston, MA 02114-2023
Phone: 617-918-1911 ext. or 1900
Fax: 617-918-1929
E-mail: owens.james@epa.gov

Bill Painter
Office of Water
U.S. Environmental Protection Agency
1200 Pennsylvania Avenue, NW
Washington, DC 20460
Phone: Not Provided
Fax: Not Provided
E-mail: Not Provided

Quentin Pair
Trail Attorney
Environmental Enforcement Section
Environment & Natural Resources Division
U.S.Department of Justice
P.O. Box 7611
Washington, DC 20044-7611
Phone: 202-514-1999
Fax: 202-514-2583
E-mail: quentin.pair@usdoj.gov

Luis E. Palacios
Vice President
Creative Concepts, Environmental Research &
Development
613 Ave Ponce de Leon, Suite 206
San Juan, 00917-4801
Phone: 787-763-9013
Fax: 787-763-9013
E-mail: lcdo.luispalacios@abanet.org

Sonia Palacios
Creative Concepts, Environmental Research &
Development
San Juan, Puerto Rico 00917
Phone: 787-760-5665
Fax: Not Provided
E-mail: Not Provided

Louis Paley
Office of Planning and Policy Analysis
Office of Enforcement and Compliance
Assurance
U.S. Environmental Protection Agency
1200 Pennsylvania Avenue, NW, (MC 2201A)
Washington, DC 20460
Phone: 202-564-2613
Fax: 202-501-0284
E-mail: paley.louis@epa.gov

Romel L. Pascual
Regional Enviornmental Justice Team Leader
Environmental Justice Office
Region 9
U.S. Environmental Protection Agency
75 Hawthorne Street, CMD-6
San Francisco, CA 94105
Phone: 415-744-1212
Fax: 415-744-1598
E-mail: pascual.romel@epamail.epa.gov

Manuel Pastor
Universtiy of California- Santa Cruz
Address Not Provided

Phone: 831-459-5919
Fax: Not Provided
E-mail: Not Provided

Shirley Pate
Office of Enforcement Capacity and Outreach
Office of Enforcement and Compliance
Assurance
U.S. Environmental Protection Agency
1200 Pennsylvania Avenue, NW, (MC 2201A)
Washington, DC 20460
Phone: 202-564-2607
Fax: 202-501-0284
E-mail: pate.shirley@epa.gov

Dorothy Patton
Office of Science Policy
Office of Research and Development
U.S. Environmental Protection Agency
1200 Pennsylvania Avenue, NW, (MC 8105)
Washington, DC 20460
Phone: Not Provided
Fax: 202-564-6705
E-mail: Not Provided

Marinelle Payton
Environmental-Occupational Medicine
School of Public Health
Harvard University Medical School
134 Marlborough Street
Boston, MA 02116
Phone: 617-525-2731
Fax: 617-731-1451
E-mail: remar@gauss.bwh.harvard.edu

Sonia Peters
Office of Environmental Justice
Office of Enforcement and Compliance
Assurance
U.S. Environmental Protection Agency
1200 Pennsylvania Avenue, NW, (MC 2201A)
Washington, DC 20460
Phone: 202-564-2634
Fax: 202-501-0740
E-mail: peters.sonia@epa.gov

Erika Petrovich
Special Assistant
Region 2
U.S. Environmental Protection Agency
290 Broadway
New York, NY 10007-1866
Phone: 212-637-5036
Fax: 212-637-5024
E-mail: Not Provided

Pamela Phillips
Superfund Division
Region 6
U.S. Environmental Protection Agency
1445 Ross Avenue, Suite 1200
Dallas, TX 75202-2733
Phone: 214-665-6701
Fax: 214-665-7330
E-mail: phillips.pamela@epa.gov

Janet Phoenix
Manager
Northeast Environmental Justice Network
1025 Connecticut Avenue, NW, Suite 1200
Washington, DC 20036
Phone: 202-974-2474
Fax: 202-659-1192
E-mail: phoenixj@nsc.org

Victoria Plata
Region 10
U.S. Environmental Protection Agency
1200 Sixth Avenue (CEJ-163)
Seattle, WA 98101
Phone: 206-553-8580
Fax: 206-553-7151
E-mail: Not Provided

Jerry Poje
Chemical Safety and Hazard Investigation
Board
Address Not Provided

Phone: Not Provided
Fax: Not Provided
E-mail: Not Provided

Carlos Porras
Communities for a Better Environment
605 West Olympic Boulevard, Suite 850
Los Angeles, CA 90015
Phone: 213-486-5114 ext. 109
Fax: 213-486-5139
E-mail: lacausala@aol.com

Gerald Prout
Director
Regulatory Affairs
FMC Corporation
1667 K Street, NW, Suite 400
Washington, DC 20006
Phone: 202-956-5209
Fax: 202-956-5235
E-mail: jerry_prout@fmc.com

Idaho Purce
INEEL Health E.S.
448 N. 6th Street
Pocatello, ID 83201
Phone: 208-232-8297
Fax: 208-232-0768
E-mail: johnpurce@aol.com

Yale Rabin
Yale Rabin Planning Consultant
6 Farrar Street
Cambridge, MA 02138
Phone: 617-661-0037
Fax: 617-661-8697
E-mail: Not Provided

Connie Raines
Manager
Environmental Justice and Community Liaison
Program
Region 4
U.S. Environmental Protection Agency
61 Forsyth Street, SW
Atlanta, GA 30303-3104
Phone: 404-562-9671
Fax: 404-562-9664
E-mail: raines.connie@epa.gov

Oscar Ramirez, Jr.
Deputy Director, Water Division
Region 6
U.S. Environmental Protection Agency
1445 Ross Avenue, Suite 1200, (6WQ-D)
Dallas, TX 75202-2733
Phone: 214-665-7390
Fax: 214-665-7373
E-mail: ramirez.oscar@epa.gov

Rosa Ramos
Community Leader
Community of Catano Against Pollution
La Marina Avenue, Mf 6, Marina Bahia
Catano, 00962
Phone: 787-788-0837
Fax: 787-788-0837
E-mail: rosah@coqui.net

Karen Randolph
Office of Solid Waste/PSPD
Office of Solid Waste and Emergency
Response
U.S. Environmental Protection Agency
1200 Pennsylvania Avenue, NW, (MC 5303W)
Washington, DC 20460
Phone: 703-308-8651
Fax: 703-308-8617
E-mail: randolph.karen@epamail.epa.gov

Arthur Ray
Deputy Secretary
Maryland Department of the Environment
2500 Broening Highway
Baltimore, MD 21224
Phone: 410-631-3086
Fax: 410-631-3888
E-mail: aray@mde.state.md.us

Doretta Reaves
Public Liaison Specialist
Office of Communications, Education and
Public Affairs
U.S. Environmental Protection Agency
1200 Pennsylvania Avenue, NW, (MC 1702)
Washington, DC 20460
Phone: 202-260-3534
Fax: 202-260-0130
E-mail: reaves.doretta@epamail.epa.gov

Deldi Reyes
Region 8
U.S. Environmental Protection Agency
999 18th Street, Suite 500
Denver, CO 80202-2466
Phone: 303-312-6055
Fax: 303-312-6409
E-mail: reyes.deldi@epamail.epa.gov

Margie F. Richard
President
Concerned Citizens of Norco
28 Washington Street
Norco, LA 70079
Phone: 225-764-8135
Fax: 225-488-3081
E-mail: Not Provided

John Ridgway
Washington State Department of Ecology
P.O. Box 47659
Olympia, WA 98504-7659
Phone: 360-407-6713
Fax: 360-407-6715
E-mail: jrid461@ecy.wa.gov

Clifford Roberts
St. James Citizens for Jobs and the
Environment
P.O. Box 162
Convent, LA 70723
Phone: 225-562-3671
Fax: Not Provided
E-mail: pacellnp@eatel.net

Dennis Roberts, II
Business Development Manager
Advanced Resources Technologies, Inc.
105 Oronoco Street
Alexandria, VA 22314
Phone: 703-836-8811
Fax: 703-683-8055
E-mail: dennis.roberts@team-arti.com

Gloria W. Roberts
St. James Citizens for Jobs and the
Environment
P.O. Box 162
Convent, LA 70723
Phone: 225-562-3671
Fax: Not Provided
E-mail: pacellnp@eatel.net

Avis Robinson
Deputy Office Director
Office of Policy and Reinvention
Office of Policy
U.S. Environmental Protection Agency
1200 Pennsylvania Avenue, NW
Washington, DC 20460
Phone: 202-260-9147
Fax: 202-401-0454
E-mail: robinson.avis@epa.gov

Leonard Robinson
TAMCO
12459 Arrow Highway
P.O. Box 325
Rancho Cucamonga, CA 91739
Phone: 909-899-0631 Ext.203
Fax: 909-899-1910
E-mail: lrobinson@gte.net

James Rollins
819 7th Street, NW Suite 400
Washington, DC 20001
Phone: 202-833-8940
Fax: 202-833-8945
E-mail: jerdlins@819eagle.com

Angela Rooney
Ward 5 Coalition for Environmental Justice
3425 14th Street, NE
Washington, DC 20017
Phone: 202-526-4592
Fax: Not Provided
E-mail: Not Provided

Caren Rothstein
Office of Pollution Prevention and Toxics
Office of Prevention, Pesticides, and Toxic
Substances
U.S. Environmental Protection Agency
1200 Pennsylvania Avenue, NW, (MC 7405)
Washington, DC 20460
Phone: 202-260-0065
Fax: 202-260-1847
E-mail: rothstein.caren@epa.gov

Margaret Round
Consultant
Clean Air Task Force
104 Farquhar Street
Roslindale, MA 02131
Phone: 617-325-4974
Fax: 617-325-7384
E-mail: margaret.round@prodigy.net

Jeffrey Ruch
Public Employees for Environmental
Responsibility
2001 S street, NW, Suite 570
Washington, DC 20009
Phone: 202-265-7337
Fax: 202-265-4192
E-mail: jruch@peer.org

Carol Rushin
ARA-ECEJ
Region 8
U.S. Environmental Protection Agency
999 18th Street, Suite 500
Denver, CO 80202-2466
Phone: 303-312-7028
Fax: 303-312-6191
E-mail: rushin.carol@epamail.epa.gov

Alberto Saldamando
General Counsel
International Indian Treaty Council
2390 Mission Street, Suite 301
San Francisco, CA 94110
Phone: 415-641-4482
Fax: 415-641-1298
E-mail: iitc@igc.apc.org

J. Gilbert Sanchez
Tribal Environmental Watch Alliance
Rt. 5, Box 442-B
Espanola, NM 87532
Phone: 505-747-7100
Fax: 505-747-7100
E-mail: tewawn@la-tierra.com

Mavis M. Sanders
Office of Civil Rights
U.S. Environmental Protection Agency
1200 Pennsylvania Avenue, NW, (MC 1201)
Washington, DC 20460
Phone: 202-260-5356
Fax: 202-260-4580
E-mail: sanders.mavis@epa.com

William H. Sanders, III
Director
Office of Pollution Prevention and Toxics
Office of Prevention, Pesticides, and Toxic
Substances
U.S. Environmental Protection Agency
1200 Pennsylvania Avenue, NW, (MC 7401)
Washington, DC 20460
Phone: 202-260-3810
Fax: 202-260-0575
E-mail: sanders.william@epa.gov

Sonya Sasseville
Permits and State Programs Division
Office of Solid Waste and Emergency
Response
U.S. Environmental Protection Agency
1200 Pennsylvania Avenue, NW (MC 5303W)
Washington, DC 20460
Phone: 202-308-8648
Fax: 202-308-8638
E-mail: sasseville.sonya@epa.gov

Barbara Sattler
University of Maryland - School of Nursing
655 W. Lombard Street, Room 665
Baltimore, MD 21201
Phone: 410-706-1849
Fax: 410-706-0295
E-mail: bsattler@ehec.umaryland.edu

Maria Sayoe
Office of International Affairs
U.S. Environmental Protection Agency
1200 Pennsylvania Avenue, NW, (MC 20460)
Washington, DC 20460
Phone: 202-564-6433
Fax: 202-565-2412
E-mail: sayoe.maria@epa.gov

Jim Schulman
Executive Director
SCI
631 E Street, NE
Washington, DC 20002
Phone: 202-544-0069
Fax: 202-544-9460
E-mail: jschulman@igc.org

Antoinette G. Sebastian
Senior Environmental Policy Analyst
Community Planning and Development
U.S. Department of Housing and Urban
Development
451 7th Street, SW, Room 7248
Washington, DC 20410
Phone: 202-708-0614 ext. 4458
Fax: 202-708-3363
E-mail: antoinette_sebastian@hud.gov

Mary Settle
Office of Environmental Justice
Office of Enforcement and Compliance
Assurance
U.S. Environmental Protection Agency
1200 Pennsylvania Avenue, NW, (MC 2201A)
Washington, DC 20460
Phone: 202-564-2594
Fax: 202-501-0740
E-mail: settle.mary@epa.gov

Michael Shapiro
Deputy Assistant Adminisrator
Office of Solid Waste and Emergency
Response
U.S. Environmental Protection Agency
1200 Pennsylvania Avenue, NW, (MC 5101)
Washington, DC 20460
Phone: 202-260-4610
Fax: 202-260-3527
E-mail: shapiro.miike@epamail.epa.gov

Sally L. Shaver
Office of Air and Radiation
U.S. Environmental Protection Agency
(MD-13)
Research Triangle Park, NC 27711
Phone: 919-541-5572
Fax: 919-541-0072
E-mail: shaver.sally@epa.gov

Christian Shaw
Legislative Assistant
NPRADC
1899 L Street, NW Suite 1000
Washington, DC 20036
Phone: 202-457-0480
Fax: 202-457-0486
E-mail: christian_shaw@npradc.org

Peggy M. Shepard
Executive Director
West Harlem Environmental Action, Inc.
271 West 125th Street, Suite 211
New York, NY 10027
Phone: 212-961-1000 ext. 303
Fax: 212-961-1015
E-mail: wheact@igc.org

Wendy Shepherd
North Carolina Department of Environment
and Natural Resources
401 Oberlin Road, Suite 150
Raleigh, NC 27605
Phone: 919-733-0692
Fax: 919-733-4810
E-mail: wendy.shepherd@ncmail.net

Robert Shinn
Commissioner
Department of Environmental Justice
New Jersey Department of Environment
Protection
401 E. State Street, P.O. Box 402, 7th Floor
Trenton, NJ 08625
Phone: 609-292-2885
Fax: 609-292-7695
E-mail: rshinn@dep.state.nj.us

Kris Shurr
Region 8
U.S. Environmental Protection Agency
999 18th Street, Suite 500
Denver, CO 80202-2466
Phone: 303-312-6139
Fax: 303-312-6064
E-mail: shurr.kris@epamail.epa.gov

Virinder Singh
Renewable Energy Policy Project
1612 K Street, NW, Suite 410
Washington, DC 20006
Phone: 202-293-1197
Fax: 202-293-5857
E-mail: virinders@repp.org

Damu Imara Smith
Southern Regional Representative
Greenpeace USA
1436 U Street, NW
Washington, DC 20009
Phone: 202-319-2410
Fax: 202-462-4507
E-mail: damu.smith@wdc.greenpeace.org

Linda K. Smith
Associate Director For Resources
Management
Office of Environmental Justice
Office of Enforcement and Compliance
Assurance
U.S. Environmental Protection Agency
1200 Pennsylvania Avenue, NW, (MC 2201A)
Washington, DC 20460
Phone: 202-564-2602
Fax: 202-501-1162
E-mail: smith.linda@epa.gov

Joe Solis
Region 7
U.S. Environmental Protection Agency
901 North 5th Street
Kansas City, KS 64108
Phone: Not Provided
Fax: Not Provided
E-mail: Not Provided

Scot Spencer
Transportation Specialist
Environmental Defense Fund
1875 Connecticut Avenue, Suite 1016
Washington, DC 21016
Phone: 202-387-3500
Fax: 202-234-6049
E-mail: scot_spencer@edf.org

Moses Squeochs
Yakama Nation
P.O. Box 151, Fort Road
Toppenish, WA 98948
Phone: 509-865-5121
Fax: 509-865-5522
E-mail: mos6@yakama.com

Jane Stahl
State of Connecticut
79 Elm Street
Hartford, CT 06106-5127
Phone: 860-424-3009
Fax: 860-424-4054
E-mail: jane.stahl@po.state.ct.us

Mathy V. Stanislaus
Director
Environmental Compliance
Enviro-Sciences, Inc.
199 Arlington Place
Staten Island, NY 10303
Phone: 718-448-7916 ext. 1246
Fax: 718-448-8666
E-mail: mstanisl@concentric.net

John Stanton
Associate Editor
Inside EPA
1225 Jefferson Davis Highway, Suite 1400
Arlington, VA 22202
Phone: 703-416-8536
Fax: 703-416-8543
E-mail: john.stanton@iwpnews.com

Michael Steinberg
Morgan, Lewis and Bockius
1800 M Street, NW
Washington, DC 20036
Phone: 202-467-7000
Fax: 202-467-7176
E-mail: stei7141@mlb.com

Juanita Stewart
President
North Baton Rouge Environmental Association
P.O. Box 781
Baker, LA 70704
Phone: 225-774-7143
Fax: Not Provided
E-mail: Not Provided

Lora Strine
Policy and Program Evaluation Division
Office of Enforcement and Compliance
Assurance
U.S. Environmental Protection Agency
1200 Pennsylvania Avenue, NW, (MC 2273A)
Washington, DC 20460
Phone: 202-564-6077
Fax: 202-564-0074
E-mail: strine.lora@epa.gov

Dean Suagee
Vermont Law School
Chelsea Street
South Royalton, VT 05068
Phone: 802-763-8303 ext. 2341
Fax: 802-763-2940
E-mail: dsuagee@vermontlaw.edu

Bill Swaney
Environmental Division Manager
Confederated Salish and Kootnai Tribes
P.O. Box 278
Pablo, MT 59855-0278
Phone: 406-675-2700
Fax: 406-675-2713
E-mail: billys@cskt.org

Charles Swiden
President of Board
Environmental Crisis Center
1936 East 30th Street
Baltimore, MD 21218
Phone: 410-235-7110
Fax: Not Provided
E-mail: not provided

Nicholas Targ
Counsel
Office of Environmental Justice
Office of Enforcement and Compliance
Assurance
U.S. Environmental Protection Agency
1200 Pennsylvania Avenue, NW, (MC 2201A)
Washington, DC 20460
Phone: 202-564-2406
Fax: 202-501-0740
E-mail: targ.nicholas@epa.gov

Michael Taylor
Vita Nuova
97 Head of Meadow
Newton, CT 06470
Phone: 203-270-3413
Fax: 203-270-3422
E-mail: taylorm@pcnet.com

Christopher Thomas
Office of Enforcement and Compliance
Environmental Justice
Region 3
U.S. Environmental Protection Agency
1650 Arch Street
Philadelphia, PA 19103-2029
Phone: 215-814-5555
Fax: 215-814-2905
E-mail: thomas.chris@epamail.epa.gov

Doreen E. Thompson
Chief
Office of Enforcement and Regulatory
Compliance
Office of Enforcement and Compliance
Assurance
U.S. Environmental Protection Agency
51 North Street, NE, 6th Floor
Washington, DC 20003
Phone: 202-535-2505
Fax: 202-535-1359
E-mail: Not Provided

James L. Thompson, Jr.
Office of Criminal Enforcement
Region 3
U.S. Environmental Protection Agency
1650 Arch Street, (3CE00)
Philadelphia, PA 19107-2029
Phone: 215-814-2374
Fax: 215-814-2383
E-mail: thompson.james@epa.gov

Joan Thurman
Office of Water
U.S. Environmental Protection Agency
1200 Pennsylvania Avenue, NW, (MC 4305)
Washington, DC 20460
Phone: 202-564-4497
Fax: Not Provided
E-mail: Not Provided

Francisco A. Tomei-Torres
Minority Health Program Specialist
Agency for Toxic Substances and Disease
Registry
1600 Clifton Road, Mail stop E28
Atlanta, GA 30333
Phone: 404-639-5060
Fax: 404-639-5063
E-mail: fbt3@cdc.gov

Gerald Torres
University of Texas Law School
727 East Dean Keeton, Room 3266
Austin, TX 78705
Phone: 512-471-2680
Fax: 512-471-6988
E-mail: gtorres@mail.law.utexas.edu

Arthur A. Totten
Office of Enforcement and Compliance
Assurance
U.S. Environmental Protection Agency
1200 Pennsylvania Avenue, NW, (MC 2252A)
Washington, DC 20460
Phone: 202-564-7164
Fax: 202-501-0072
E-mail: totten.arthur@epa.gov

Connie Tucker
Executive Director
Southern Organizing Committee for Economic
and Social Justice
P.O. Box 10518
Atlanta, GA 30310
Phone: 404-755-2855
Fax: 404-755-0575
E-mail: socejp@igc.apc.org

Robin Turner
Joint Center for Political and Economic Studies
1090 Vermont Avenue, Northwest
Suite 1100
Washington, DC 20005
Phone: 202-789-3500
Fax: 202-789-6390
E-mail: rturner@jointcenter.org

Haywood Turrentine
Laborers Education Training Trust Fund
500 Lancaster Pike
Exton, PA 19341
Phone: 610-524-0404
Fax: 610-524-6411
E-mail: hlj1@aol.com

Delta Enid Valente
Project Manager
Farm Worker Health
Office of Prevention, Pesticides, and Toxic
Substances
U.S. Environmental Protection Agency
1200 Pennsylvania Avenue, NW, (MC 7506C)
Washington, DC 20460
Phone: 703-305-7164
Fax: 703-308-2962
E-mail: valente.delta@epa.gov

Alice Walker
Program Analyst
Office of Water
U.S. Environmental Protection Agency
1200 Pennsylvania Avenue, NW, (MC 4102)
Washington, DC 20460
Phone: 202-260-1919
Fax: 202-269-3597
E-mail: walker.alice@epa.gov

Nathalie Walker
Earthjustice Legal Defense Fund
400 Magazine Street, Suite 401
New Orleans, LA 70130
Phone: 504-522-1394
Fax: 504-566-7242
E-mail: nwalker@earthjustice.org

Matt Ward
National Association of Local Government
Environmental Professionals
1350 New York Avenue, NW
Washington, DC 20005
Phone: 202-879-4093
Fax: 202-393-2866
E-mail: matt.ward@spiegelmcd.com

Roger K. Ward
Office of the Secretary
Louisiana Department of Environmental
Qualilty
P.O. Box 82263
Baton Rouge, LA 70884
Phone: 225-765-0741
Fax: 225-765-0746
E-mail: roger_w@deq.state.la.us

Oliver L. Warnsley
Superfund Division
Region 5
U.S. Environmental Protection Agency
77 West Jackson Boulevard (SR-6J)
Chicago, IL 60604
Phone: 312-886-0442
Fax: 312-886-4071
E-mail: warnsley.oliver@epa.gov

Barbara Warren
Consumer Policy Institute of the Consumers
Union
101 Truman Avenue
Yonkers, NY 10703
Phone: 718-984-6446
Fax: 718-984-0500
E-mail: warrenba@email.msn.com

Joan Warren
Office of Water
U.S. Environmental Protection Agency
1200 Pennsylvania Avenue, NW
Washington, SDC 20460
Phone: Not Provided
Fax: Not Provided
E-mail: Not Provided

Daniel Wartenberg
Professor
EOHSI
170 Frelinghousen House
Piscataway, NJ 08859
Phone: 732-445-0197
Fax: 732-445-0784
E-mail: dew@eohsi.rutgers.edu

David Wawer
Chemical Manufacturers Association
1300 Wilson Boulevard
Arlington, VA 22209
Phone: 703-741-5161
Fax: 703-741-6161
E-mail: david_wawer@cmahq.com

Suzanne E. Wells
Director
Community Involvement and Outreach Center
Superfund Program
U.S. Environmental Protection Agency
1200 Pennsylvania Avenue, NW, (MC 5204G)
Washington, DC 20460
Phone: 703-603-8863
Fax: 703-603-9100
E-mail: wells.suzanne@epa.gov

Chen H. Wen
Program Analyst
Office of Pollution Prevention and Toxic
Substances
Office of Prevention, Pesticides, and Toxic
Substances
U.S. Environmental Protection Agency
1200 Pennsylvania Avenue, NW, (MC 7404)
Washington, DC 20460
Phone: 202-260-4109
Fax: 202-260-0178
E-mail: wen.chen@epamail.gov

Frank Wennin
Consultant
Environment Crisis Center
2541 St. Paul Street
Baltimore, MD 21224
Phone: 410-662-7758
Fax: Not Provided
E-mail: Not Provided

Carol A. Wettstein
Environmental Justice Coordinator
U.S. Forest Service
U.S. Department of Agriculture
P.O. Box 96090
Washington, DC 20090-6090
Phone: 202-205-1588
Fax: 202-205-1174
E-mail: cwettstein/wo@fs.fed.us

Angele C. White
ICMA
777 North Capitol Street, NE, Suite 500
Washington, DC 20002
Phone: 202-962-3563
Fax: 202-962-3500
E-mail: awhite@icma.org

Damon Whitehead
Staff Attorney
Lawyer's Committee For Civil Rights Under
the Law
1450 G Street, NW, Suite 400
Washington, DC 20005
Phone: 202-662-8600
Fax: 202-783-5113
E-mail: dwhitehe@lawyerscomm.org

Amina Wilkins
Environmental Scientist
National Center for Environmental Assessment
Office of Research and Development
U.S. Environmental Protection Agency
1200 Pennsylvania Avenue, NW, (MC 8623)
Washington, DC 20460
Phone: 202-564-3256
Fax: 202-565-0076
E-mail: wilkins.amina@epamail.epa.gov

Margaret Williams
President
Citizens Against Toxic Exposure
6400 Marianna Drive
Pensacola, FL 32504
Phone: 904-494-2601
Fax: 904-479-2044
E-mail: Not Provided

Lillian A. Wilmore
Director
(Kiowa heritage)
Native Ecology Initiative
P.O. Box 470829
Brookline Village, MA 02447-0829
Phone: 617-232-5742
Fax: 617-277-1656
E-mail: naecology@aol.com

J. Wil Wilson
Senior Scientist
Office of Air and Radiation
U.S. Environmental Protection Agency
1200 Pennsylvania Avenue, NW, (MC 6101)
Washington, DC 20460
Phone: 202-564-1954
Fax: 202-564-1549
E-mail: wil wilson@epa.gov.com

Mary Wilson
Region 6
U.S. Environmental Protection Agency
1445 Ross Avenue, Suite 1200, (6MD-D)
Dallas, TX 75202
Phone: 214-665-6439
Fax: 214-665-8072
E-mail: mwilson@epamail.epa.gov

Nancy Wilson
Office of Solid Waste and Emergency
Response
U.S. Environmental Protection Agency
1200 Pennsylvania Avenue, NW, (MC 5104)
Washington, DC 20460
Phone: Not Provided
Fax: Not Provided
E-mail: Not Provided

Anna Marie Wood
Senior Regulatory Impact Analyst
Office of Enforcement and Compliance
Office of Air and Radiation
U.S. Environmental Protection Agency
1200 Pennsylvania Avenue, NW, (MC 6103A)
Washington, DC 20164
Phone: 202-564-1664
Fax: 202-564-1554
E-mail: wood.anna@epa.gov

James Woolford
Director, Federal Facilities Restoration and
Reuse Office
Office of Solid Waste
Office of Solid Waste and Emergency
Response
U.S. Environmental Protection Agency
1200 Pennsylvania Avenue, NW, (MC 5101)
Washington, DC 20460
Phone: 202-260-1606
Fax: 202-260-3527
E-mail: Not Provided

Linda Woolley
Principal
LegisLaw
1115 Connecticut Avenue, NW, 500
Washington, DC 20036
Phone: 202-466-4840
Fax: 202-466-4841
E-mail: legislaw@aol.com

Eddie L. Wright
Environmental Analyst
Waste Management Division
Region 4
U.S. Environmental Protection Agency
61 Forsyth Street, SW
Atlanta, GA 30303-3104
Phone: 404-562-8669
Fax: 404-562-8628
E-mail: wright.eddie@epa.gov

George Wyeth
Senior Counsel
Office of Reinvention Policy
Office of the Administrator
U.S. Environmental Protection Agency
1200 Pennsylvania Avenue, NW, (MC 1803)
Washington, DC 20460
Phone: 202-260-7726
Fax: Not Provided
E-mail: wyeth.george@epa.gov

Michelle Xenox
Shundahai Network
5007 Elmhurst Lane
Las Vegas, NV 89108
Phone: 702-647-3095
Fax: 702-547-9385
E-mail: shundahai@shundahai.org

Gerald H. Yamada
Attorney
Paul, Hastings, Janofsky and Walker LLP
1200 Pennsylvania Avenue, NW, 10th Floor
Washington, DC 20004
Phone: 202-508-9573
Fax: 202-508-9700
E-mail: ghyamada@phjw.com

Marianne Yamaguchi
Director
Santa Monica Bay Restoration Project
320 West 4th Street, Suite 200
Los Angeles, CA 90013
Phone: 213-576-6614
Fax: 213-576-6646
E-mail: myamaguc@rb4.swrcb.ca.gov

Tseming Yang
Vermont School of Law
Chelsea Street, Whitcomb House
South Royalton, VT 05068
Phone: 802-763-8303 ext. 2344
Fax: 802-763-2663
E-mail: tyang@vermontlaw.edu

Harold Yates
Senior Community Involvement Coordinator
Hazardous Site Cleanup Division
Region 3
U.S. Environmental Protection Agency
1650 Arch Street
Philadelphia, PA 19103
Phone: 215-814-5530
Fax: Not Provided
E-mail: yates.hal@epamail.epa.gov

Bill Yellowtail
Regional Administrator
Region 8
U.S. Environmental Protection Agency
999 18th Street, Suite 500
Denver, CO 80202-2466
Phone: 303-312-6308
Fax: 303-312-6882
E-mail: yellowtail.bill@epa.gov

Laura Yoshii
Deputy Regional Administrator
Cross Media Division
Region 9
U.S. Environmental Protection Agency
75 Hawthorne Street
San Francisco, CA 94105
Phone: 415-744-1001
Fax: 415-744-2499
E-mail: yoshii.laura@epa.gov

James Younger
Region 1
U.S. Environmental Protection Agency
One Congress Street, Suite 1100
Boston, MA 02114-2023
Phone: 617-918-1059
Fax: 617-918-1029
E-mail: younger.james@epamail.epa.gov

Hal Zenick
Acting Deputy Assistant Administrator
Office of Research and Development
U.S. Environmental Protection Agency
MD-87
Research Triangle Park, NC 22771
Phone: Not Provided
Fax: Not Provided
E-mail: zenick.hal@epa.gov

APPENDIX C

ENVIRONMENTAL JUSTICE IN THE PERMITTING PROCESS:
A Report from the National Environmental Justice Advisory Council's
Public meeting on Environmental Permitting - Arlington, Virginia
November 30-December 2, 1999

COMMENTS TO THE OFFICE OF AIR AND RADIATION

ON THE EPA'S DRAFT URBAN AIR TOXICS STRATEGY

April 6, 1999

Prepared by the

NATIONAL ENVIRONMENTAL JUSTICE ADVISORY COUNCIL
AIR AND WATER SUBCOMMITTEE'S
URBAN AIR TOXICS WORKING GROUP

Workgroup Members:
Maribel N. Nicholson-Choice, The Law Firm of Greenberg Traurig
Felice Stadler, Clean Air Network
Barbara Warren, Consumer Policy Institute–Consumer Union
Damon P. Whitehead, Workgroup Chair, Lawyers Committee for Civil Rights Under Law

TABLE OF CONTENTS

INTRODUCTION

The National Environmental Justice Advisory Council's ("NEJAC") Air and Water Subcommittee authorized the creation of the Urban Air Toxics ("UAT") Working Group at its December 7, 1998 meeting in Baton Rouge, Louisiana. The UAT Working Group has been charged to examine the Draft Urban Air Toxics Strategy ("Urban Air Strategy"), published by the United States Environmental Protection Agency ("EPA" or "Agency"), and to develop recommendations for the Agency to incorporate environmental justice concerns into the Urban Air Strategy. The UAT Working Group is comprised of representatives from environmental, local government, industry, civil rights, and consumer rights organizations. The UAT Working Group worked with staff from EPA responsible for developing the Urban Air Strategy to develop an understanding of the strategy, goals, and available resources for implementation. The UAT Working Group conferred numerous times amongst itself and with EPA staff beginning January 1999. The UAT Working Group has completed its initial deliberations and hereby submits this report for EPA's consideration.

OVERVIEW

The UAT Working Group asserts that the Urban Air Strategy serves as the foundation for the agency to comprehensively address air quality in urban areas. The potential benefits of this strategy, if realized, will be an important victory for EPA, environmental justice groups, the communities they serve, and other stakeholders. An EPA analysis has demonstrated that people of color and low income populations disproportionately benefit from the stringent enforcement of the Clean Air Act ("CAA" or "Act"). Environmental Justice Annual Report, EPA 1994. Conversely, it must be true, that these same populations have suffered a disproportionate harm as a result of shortcomings in enforcement of the Act and meeting urban air quality standards. The UAT Working Group believes that the Urban Air Strategy should accomplish the goal of Section 112(k) of the Clean Air Act, to achieve measurable and significant air quality improvements in urban areas, and that this and other important environmental justice issues, such as assessing cumulative impacts and achieving actual risk reductions are attainable. However, to achieve the goals of the Urban Air Strategy and the other broader concerns, EPA must realize and use its immense legal authority under all statutes within its jurisdiction. Proper implementation of the Urban Air Strategy, including effective participation by environmental justice advocates, communities, and other

3

stakeholders, holds a lot of promise; however, a weak, poorly funded and unfocused strategy will mean many more years with few, if any, measurable results.

THE EPA'S DRAFT INTEGRATED URBAN AIR TOXICS STRATEGY

EPA published the Urban Air Strategy on September 1, 1998. EPA is scheduled to published a final strategy by June 18, 1999. The EPA's Urban Air Strategy is intended to reduce air toxic emissions in urban areas through regulatory and voluntary programs. The Urban Air Strategy is a fulfillment of rulemaking Docket Number 97-44. EPA has stated that the goal of the Urban Air Strategy is to protect public health and the environment from toxic air pollutants. This goal should be pursued with care to avoid creating problems, and interfering with job creation and economic revitalization initiatives of urban communities. Although the Urban Air Strategy is not a rule, the EPA expects the Urban Air Strategy to be the basis for new rules regulating toxic air emissions in urban areas. One of the major challenges for EPA will be to truly integrate the Urban Air Strategy with existing federal air programs, such as the Maximum Achievable Control Technology (MACT) program and rulemaking initiatives.

SUMMARY OF ISSUES

The UAT Working Group will address several core issues in this report. They include:

1.   How should EPA integrate the Urban Air Strategy with the MACT program and other rule-making initiatives.

2.   How should EPA define "urban" for purposes of the Urban Air Strategy.

3.   How should EPA use the Cumulative Exposure Project ("CEP") data.

4.   How should air monitoring initiatives be coordinated among EPA, states, and local governments.

5.   Should EPA list new Hazardous Air Pollutants ("HAPs") and new sources in the Urban Air Strategy.

6.   What is the design and scope of a model local air program that examines environmental justice issues in urban areas.

7.   How should community input be solicited and incorporated into the Urban Air Strategy to supplement data used by EPA to identify areas of concern in urban areas.

8.   How should EPA measure and quantify risk reduction.

9.   How should EPA conduct a cumulative impact analysis in urban areas.

10.   How should EPA integrate residual risk principles in the Urban Air Strategy.

11.   Should EPA conduct health surveillance as part of implementing the Urban Air Strategy.

Consensus Principles

5

1.   The UAT Working Group agrees that discrimination on the basis of race, color, or national origin is illegal and unjust.

2.   The UAT Working Group agrees that EPA should identify, promote and ensure meaningful participation by all stakeholders.

3.   The UAT Working Group recognizes that cumulative impacts in urban areas should be addressed effectively.

4.   The UAT Working Group recognizes that cumulative exposure and synergistic health effects are important concerns of urban areas.

5.   The UAT Working Group agrees that EPA should continue to consult with all affected stakeholders in regard to finalizing the Urban Air Strategy.

6.   The UAT Working Group agrees that the Urban Air Strategy should be truly integrated with other programs and rulemaking.

7.   The UAT Working Group agrees that the EPA should assess the public health significance of exposure of HAPs in urban areas and report that risk in a responsible and understandable anner to communities.

THE UAT WORKING GROUP'S RECOMMENDED ACTION ITEMS FOR EPA

Integrated and Comprehensive Regulation of Air Toxic Emissions

STATIONARY SOURCES

The UAT Working Group believes the Urban Air Strategy has two main goals: to address toxic emissions from area sources that to date are largely unregulated; and, to address the mix of pollutants found in urban areas (the "urban soup"). One of the most immediate and effective means of meeting these two goals is through integrating current regulatory activities within the Agency with the implementation of the Urban Air Strategy.

A majority of the UAT Working Group believes that this can be accomplished, in part, by integrating the Urban Air Strategy into current rulemakings targeting major sources. EPA should:

1.   Gather information on area source emissions when developing new MACTs (specifically the 10-year MACTs). Consider the quantity, geographic distribution, and health significance of emissions. Apply best available technology to area sources but also make extensive use of pollution prevention options such as materials substitution. Evaluate health significance of all uncontrolled emissions of a particular HAP (including those sources and emission points not subject to the MACT, as well as area

sources not subject to a standard).

2. Integrate all EPA rulemakings with this strategy and the need to control HAPs and the corresponding health risks. All offices of EPA should evaluate the relationship between their activities and the need to comprehensively control HAPs.

3. Use authority under other statutes to adequately address all HAPs such as emissions from the use of consumer products.

4. Publish a complete list of all major and area sources of all HAP emissions with their relevant 4-digit SIC codes.

5. Conduct a review of MACT affected and unaffected facilities to determine the effectiveness of MACTs thus far in actually regulating source categories involved.

The UAT Working Group further urges that rulemaking targeting area sources to meet the goals of the Urban Air Strategy should:

1. Integrate regulation with the Title V program.

2. Require emissions statements from listed area sources.

3. Establish thresholds for emissions reporting based on toxicity of HAPs.

4. Charge an annual fee, rather than a per ton fee for area sources of HAPs.

5. Allow use of Title V fees to fund state toxics reduction programs.

6. Require all states to set Title V fees at the levels established in the Clean Air Act.

The majority of the UAT Working Group believes that it is important that for current MACT rulemakings (rules that are being developed, but have not yet been proposed), EPA ensure that the goals of the Urban Air Strategy are being met. For instance, the Industrial Combustion Coordinated Rulemaking has the potential to reduce a group of HAP emissions from thousands of small combustion sources. If the final rule does not set specific standards for key pollutants, such as mercury, EPA will miss a crucial opportunity - one that may not be regained - to regulate pollutants that adversely affect urban air quality, and will necessarily contradict the goals of the Urban Air Strategy.

The UAT Working Group believes that all rulemaking should emphasize pollution prevention practices as a means of meeting emissions standards. Existing sources using pollution prevention or toxics use reduction practices (such as materials substitution) should serve as a model, and should drive the outcome of each standard. Moreover, toxics use reduction (source reduction) should be a component of every rulemaking. It is important that major sources currently subject to existing MACT standards not

7

be targeted for additional emission reduction requirements until EPA has first considered reducing emissions from other sources.

MOBILE SOURCES

The UAT Working Group believes that EPA should evaluate the need and feasibility of new mobile source regulations as part of updating the mobile toxics inventory. As part of this effort, EPA should estimate potential reductions of tailpipe HAP emissions anticipated through full implementation of the Tier 2 and fuel sulfur rulemakings.

In addition, EPA should take advantage of current efforts to evaluate new diesel emission standards as an opportunity to begin fulfilling the Agency's objectives under the Urban Air Strategy. EPA should recommend the use of innovative technologies to reduce diesel particulate emissions, which will result in reductions of toxic hydrocarbon emissions.

The majority of the UAT Working Group believes that EPA's mobile source emissions rulemakings should evaluate emission contributions from the entire transportation, storage and distribution system for fuels for possible additional regulation. This part of the fuel system usually impacts urban centers because of the distribution of storage facilities as well as high usage in urban areas.

CEP Data

The UAT Working Group believes that the Cumulative Exposure Project (CEP) data is useful as a screening tool. The majority of the UAT Working Group believes that for the first time, EPA has valuable modeling data on projected ambient concentrations of a range of HAPs. The UAT Working Group, however, believes that the current CEP data should not be the only approach for deciding a course of action to address local toxics because the CEP data has technical limitations. Rather, the CEP data should be used by states to help prioritize local action in terms of identifying toxic concentrations, locating key emission sources, and assessing monitoring needs. It should be used as a tool by states and EPA when developing a local and nationwide toxics monitoring network. The overall objective should be employing a network of monitors in order to verify existing modeling data and generate more complete inventories.

Air Monitoring Networks

The UAT Working Group believes that air monitoring networks are an important and useful tool to assess emission reductions and high emission concentrations. The UAT Working Group asserts that more ambient monitoring for HAPs is needed, as well as assessments of exposure and health effects posed

8

by HAPs. While the CEP data provides valuable information, a comprehensive network of monitors is essential to get accurate information on specific pollutants and contributing sources. All monitoring data should be publicly available, including the draft monitoring plans. The majority of the UAT Working Group believes that EPA should pursue the following goals and objectives when developing a national toxic air monitoring program:

1. All large cities of the country should have air monitors for HAPs operating within two years. These monitors should supplement the fine particle monitors being installed. Measured pollutants from fine particle monitors (not just the speciated monitors) and the toxics monitors should be compiled and reported to the AIRS database. Toxics being measured through IMPROVE monitors should also be reported to the same database.

2. EPA should oversee the development of the toxics monitoring program to ensure that additional monitors are being strategically placed and are expanding upon existing networks rather than just being co-located with other monitors (for instance the PAMS and IMPROVE networks). EPA should encourage monitoring for different ubiquitous pollutants to get a broad national perspective as well as to allow monitoring for some pollutants likely to be of local concern. This is critical to confirm or refute the CEP modeling results.

3. HAPs selected because of local concern should have a reasonable rationale for their selection. Monitoring for various persistent bioaccumulative toxins is essential.

4. Large emissions of TRI chemicals (those not on HAP list) in a particular area may warrant ambient monitoring for those particular chemicals.

5. Large concentrations of industrial facilities in a non-urban area should also be considered for selection as part of the early network.

6. Public health researchers should be involved in the development of a toxics monitoring program, including providing input on pollutants of concern and designing the network to enable the data to be used for research purposes.

7. Assuring the public's right to know about the results must be a required element, as well as a proactive process for disseminating information.

The UAT Working Group believes that EPA should provide in the final Urban Air Strategy a description of the roles and responsibilities that will be allocated to EPA, the states, and local government in implementing an air monitoring network.

List of Sources

9

The UAT Working Group believes that due to the limited area source emissions data, the source category list is only a starting point for addressing air toxics. The list of source categories may need to be modified (through additions or deletions) as monitoring data become available. Therefore, the strategy must remain flexible to respond and regulate new sources as data become available. Moreover, the strategy must recognize the economic impact of adding particular small businesses to the area source list. Regulation under the Urban Air Strategy may not be the best and most economical manner for reducing these source emissions. Instead, EPA should consider regulation of the products used in certain small businesses such as nail shops and beauty shops. Furthermore, EPA should encourage pollution prevention and the use of alternative products by small business.

The majority of the UAT Working Group believes that before finalizing the Urban Air Strategy, EPA should revisit the draft source list. EPA should compare the draft source list to the sources identified by the State and Territorial Air Pollution Program Administrators and consider adding several key sources that were omitted from EPA's initial list, such as printers and airports. EPA, however, should not list any source for which the Agency is not prepared to use all of its authority to fully regulate.

List of Pollutants

The UAT Working Group recommends that EPA revisit the list of pollutants currently identified in the Urban Air Strategy. The UAT Working Group is concerned with the mechanism used for developing the list of priority HAPs, and believes that EPA should explain in the final Urban Air Strategy how the HAPs were identified. The UAT Working Group also recommends that EPA remain flexible with its list of priority HAPs as the program is being fully implemented. Through rigorous monitoring, a more complete inventory of HAP emissions in urban areas will be developed. EPA should rely on the updated inventory to verify that the right pollutants of concern are being targeted under the Urban Air Strategy.

The majority of the UAT Working Group recommends that EPA consider adding pollutants suggested by STAPPA, as well as polychlorinated biphenyls. If EPA is prepared to use its authority under TSCA to address pollutants emitted almost exclusively from the use of consumer products, then the EPA should list these pollutants in the final Urban Air Strategy. If EPA does not intend to address this "nonpoint" source, it may not be appropriate to list them in the Urban Air Strategy.

State Programs

The majority of the UAT Working Group believes that EPA should address consistent and pervasive exceedances of established health benchmark concentrations for a number of priority HAPs found nationally by establishing national standards.

10

The majority of the UAT Working Group believes that the EPA should signal support and offer incentives, including funding for existing and new-air toxics programs at the state level and encourage states to go beyond minimum requirements. States should be required to develop a UAT plan specific to the individual state, its urban areas and toxic hotspots. EPA should provide guidance to states and review plans to ensure accountability. States should work closely with Small Business Assistance Programs to build on information already gathered. The majority of the UAT Working Group believes that the state plans should:

1. Identify areas that the state agency will focus on for air monitoring.

2. Complete a profile of area sources concentrated in a particular area, and their emissions.

3. Quantify HAP emissions and contributing sources, and whether the source is currently regulated under a MACT, GACT, or another emission standard.

4. Identify known and potential toxic hotspots (using CEP results, ambient monitoring, TRI), and assess which communities are potentially affected, such as adjoining and downwind communities.

5. Describe in detail the full range of public participation activities planned by the agency. One specific requirement should be holding community roundtables in targeted neighborhoods.

6. Develop detailed action plans to ensure representatives from the environmental justice and community organizations are active participants in drafting the state plan.

7. Provide an opportunity for the public to petition the state and EPA for air monitoring changes, such as source category changes and hotspot attention, and require the state agency to provide a detailed response if the petition is not accepted.

The UAT Working Group urges EPA to set up a comprehensive framework to accomplish the goals of the Urban Air Strategy, but allow states flexibility in determining how to achieve the desired results. EPA can best serve this end by defining what must be accomplished and how progress will be measured in the real world.

Resources and incentives need to be made available to provide states added incentive to develop state toxics programs. Some of these may include:

1. Using the 112(l) program and providing grant allocations.

2. Using emission fees to fund portions of the program.

3. Providing new funding to states specifically for this program.

4. Include criteria in EPA's performance partnership agreements that would explicitly require states to set up toxics monitoring networks and a toxics program.

11

5. Include some requirements in the state air grants issued annually.

6. Issuing grants under the Clean Air Partnership Fund to fund state toxics programs and making this one of the selection criteria when soliciting proposals.

Areas of Concern

The UAT Working Group believes that a strategy driven solely on the identification of urban areas or geographic hotspots could cause facilities to merely move to "green fields." The majority of the UAT Working Group believes that the backbone of the overall strategy must be driven by national standards and regulations for all source categories of HAP emissions. This will avoid simply moving toxic problems elsewhere to avoid regulation.

States should address the problem of toxic hot spots in their new or existing air toxic programs. The first step in addressing this is identifying where problems exist and what steps are needed to reduce ambient concentrations of toxics. States should use CEP data as a starting point with their knowledge of area sources in a particular area, and with the intended goal of installing a dense network of monitors to develop a more complete inventory of sources contributing to the problem.

The UAT Working Group believe that pollution prevention, sustainable development and small business assistance should all be emphasized in this strategy. Environmental justice advocates and impacted communities have consistently demanded safe and economically viable alternatives to polluting industries in their communities. EPA should use a multi-program scheme such as crossing brownfield and sustainable development funding to encourage these types of developments.

The majority of the UAT Working Group believes that EPA should develop a national policy requiring close risk review prior to issuing permits to new and modified sources. There should be a national "no-degradation" policy with regards to air toxics. Given that areas throughout the U.S. already have unacceptable levels of HAP emissions, this policy would prohibit the issuance of any new permit that would allow new emissions of a similar class of pollutants in those impacted areas (e.g., if there is a cluster of cancer-causing emissions in a neighborhood, no new source emitting (probable or listed) carcinogens would be allowed). This policy needs to apply to local airsheds (neighborhoods) as well as entire metropolitan areas. The risk review must consider cumulative impacts of HAPs with a common health effect to ensure that public health does not further degrade with the increase in HAP emissions.

Measuring and Quantifying Risk Reductions

The UAT Working Group believes risk reductions are not real or quantifiable as long as they are based on inadequate measurements. Risk reductions can be a correlated measure with real reductions in emissions of hazardous air pollutants, and therefore this is the quantifiable measure that should be used. Estimates of reductions and air modeling are not adequate. Risk reductions also cannot be national in scope. This would ignore both what is mandated in the Clean Air Act and the problem of high concentrations of HAPs in urban areas.

To measure real reductions, baseline air monitoring measurements of HAPs must be established in urban communities throughout the nation. In addition, EPA must establish a more complete emissions inventory based on actual measurements (and not just emission factors) for each listed source category prior to developing an emissions standard. EPA should rely on state Small Business Assistance Programs, many of which have been working with area sources of HAPs and have been gathering emissions data from these sectors.

Risk reductions under the Urban Air Strategy need to be achieved for both priority areas being addressed in the strategy - emissions from currently unregulated area sources, and the concentrated mixture of HAPs uniquely found in urban areas. A majority of the UAT Working Group recommends to EPA as follows:

1. Collect emission statements from area sources of HAPs (working with SBAPs as much as is practicable).

2. Evaluate toxicity of various pollutants—including cancer and non-cancer effects (e.g., neurotoxins, respiratory irritants).

3. Evaluate total aggregate emissions of HAP pollutants and their toxicity for each urban area.

4. Evaluate disproportionate geographic distribution of emissions within the urban area that could lead to higher risks for particular communities.

At the same time, EPA should not just focus on current emissions. Background concentrations from reservoirs should not be ignored since many of these contaminants consist of PBTs, greatly influence the total health risk, and continue to have adverse impacts long after industrial sources are controlled.

Cumulative Impacts

The UAT Working Group believes EPA should begin conducting an assessment of the cumulative impacts of all HAPs with common health effects, such as neurotoxins, by using an additive model. If synergism is known, appropriate multiplying factors should be utilized. This will require the assistance and involvement of researchers and public health and medical professionals. Cumulative impact analysis must account for background concentrations, persistent bioaccumulative toxins, and more than known

13

current emissions. Cumulative impacts must be assessed and risk reductions achieved not just at the national and regional level, but also for smaller severely impacted communities, frequently inhabited by people of color and low income populations. Averaging out large impacts is unacceptable and not good public health practice.

Multi-pathway analysis is also important for assessing cumulative impacts.

Residual Risk

The majority of the UAT Working Group believes that the Urban Air Strategy should include a new approach for conducting residual risk. Analysis of residual risk should be comprehensive and address all HAP sources and opportunities for reducing the risks to public health. (Residual risk is more meaningful to the public if it means risks left over after all possible control strategies have been implemented.) For this reason, instead of looking narrowly at the source category currently subject to the MACT standard, EPA should look at all emission sources of a particular HAP and hold those particular sources accountable. It should then identify regulated and unregulated sources and controlled and uncontrolled emission points. If this more comprehensive approach is adopted as part of the Urban Air Strategy, then EPA should be eligible to exercise broader authority than currently is suggested under the MACT residual risk program.

In addition, rather than waiting to evaluate residual risk once a rule is finalized, EPA should conduct a pre-residual risk analysis while developing new toxic emission standards (for major, area *and* mobile sources). Analyzing all sources of a particular HAP while developing a standard will provide the agency a better assessment on whether the resulting standard will adequately reduce health risks, and how the standard should be improved to ensure risks are, in fact, reduced.

Linking Health Surveillance with Urban Air Strategy

EPA should coordinate with public health researchers when designing databases and when developing and siting a national toxics monitoring network. Traditionally, EPA does not consider health effects research when setting up these network. It's imperative that this component is incorporated through the design and installation of toxics monitors (similar to approach being taken with the PM2.5 monitoring network). States also should be required to work with public health researchers when developing its network. Any guidance, policies, assessments, or evaluations of toxic exposure initiated by EPA should be conducted in close coordination with public health researchers.

Public health policy also should be a prominent component of the national "no-degradation" policy. For example, in the case of asthma, NYC has high incidence rates for hospitalizations and deaths.

14

Even without linking air pollutants with the incidence of disease, based on two separate sets of knowledge—knowledge of disease rates and knowledge of air pollution— air quality officials should act to reduce air pollutants that are respiratory irritants so that asthma is not exacerbated.

Public Participation and Environmental Justice

The UAT Working Group believes that EPA should develop national policy specifying how federal and states agencies will ensure ongoing, meaningful involvement by the environmental justice advocates, community groups, and other stakeholders as the Urban Air Strategy is implemented. The policy should be explicit in how EPA will guarantee participation in all areas of the Urban Air Strategy such as research, air monitoring, health surveillance.

In addition, the policy should outline state requirements for:

1. Developing a process for continuously consulting communities.
2. Providing assistance needed to guarantee meaningful involvement.
3. Develop protocol for distributing announcements regarding upcoming hearings and public meetings to be sensitive to particular community needs.
4. Identify key civic associations that should be brought into the process, and can play a role in reaching out to communities.
5. Establish a citizen task force to oversee the development and implementation of the state's toxics program.
6. Develop a plan to assess the public health significance of exposure to HAPs in urban areas and to report risk in a responsible and understandable manner to communities.

Phase-In of the Urban Air Strategy

The UAT Working Group believes that critical data gaps exist that can jeopardize the integrity of the Urban Air Strategy. It is recommended that EPA implement a national air toxics program in distinct steps as it continues to address these gaps, and seek stakeholder input at each stage of the process. In addition to those suggested above, the following near- and long-term actions are proposed:

Near Term Actions

1. Establish a process for continuing dialogue with environmental justice advocates, community organizations, state and local agencies, public health researchers, industry and other stakeholders continuously throughout the phase-in of the program. Solicit interest in receiving regular notices of new draft proposals, updates on progress, and schedule for meetings. Set up a framework for this kind of continuing input in the Urban Air Strategy to be released in June.

15

2.   Develop a plan for providing the public with the CEP information, such as through community roundtables, conferences, educational materials, Internet, and EPA should act as a clearinghouse for information.

3.   Carefully consider the budgetary needs of EPA for the Urban Air Strategy as well as for states, so that budget requests can be incorporated into the federal budget process. Make budget recommendations and rationale available to interested parties.

4.   Develop a plan to fill remaining data gaps, such as research on area source emissions.

5.   Compare CEP information with actual monitoring data in different areas of the country, and ensure that this information is available to the public.

6.   Plan air monitoring network with involvement of all identified in number 1 above. Get air monitoring set up immediately in the twenty most populous cities.

7.   Identify scientific, public health and technical questions and set up an advisory board to address these questions and oversee implementation of the Urban Air Strategy.

8.   Carefully consider the budgetary needs and fund research for assessment of the public health significance of exposure to HAPs in urban areas.

9.   Carefully consider the budgetary needs and fund air state monitoring networks and air toxic programs.

10.   EPA should fully integrate all EPA rulemaking and the MACT program in the Urban Air Strategy to avoid duplicative regulation of the same HAPs and sources.

11.   EPA should conduct research requiring the reduction of risk and emission accomplished by existing rules prior to considering the adoption of additional rules based on the Urban Air Strategy.

Intermediate and Ongoing Actions

1.   Formalize the framework for continued input by making available research plans for comment; by incorporating public comment in the research plans; by gathering the needed data and information, evaluating it with outside parties and using it to set priorities; by continuing to develop and evaluate the progress of the program with input from the affected public and scientific advisors; and by measuring progress with quantifiable measures.

2.   Develop rules for acting on CEP data if verified by monitoring data in sufficient areas of the country.

3.   Work with states, locals and the public to develop plans for urban areas and other hotspots. As part of this effort gather information on brownfield sites, and other potential areas of concern.

4.   Collect and evaluate air monitoring data on a regular basis, and update pollutant and source category

16

lists as new information is obtained.

CONCLUSION

This report provides the initial recommendations of the UAT Working Group. We will provide or modify our comments as additional information becomes available, and at a minimum, will review and provide recommendations on the final Urban Air Strategy.